Inside
America
Scenes of
Everyday
Life

Martha E. Kendall

Inside America is dedicated with much love to Joe Weed.   As this project grew from being mine to ours, it kept on getting better—just like so many things in my life.

ISBN 0-945783-07-8

Highland Publishing

P. O. Box 554
Los Gatos, CA 95031-0554
U.S.A.
fax (408) 353-3388
phone (408) 353-5756
esl@highlandpublishing.com

Inside America
Scenes of Everyday Life

Preface

Preface

Inside America develops high-intermediate and advanced ESL students' listening-speaking skills as they learn about life in the United States. It is designed to be practical, learner-centered, flexible and easy to use. The video and book provide varied learning options; users may select those most appropriate for their needs and interests. The units are organized thematically, and they can be studied in any order.

The video contains thirteen units, each about fifteen minutes long. The units begin and end with a candid interview in natural, authentic speech. Following the introductory interview, each unit presents everyday people and places. The narration explains the norms of American culture that the scenes illustrate.

Students use the book to improve their listening comprehension, increase their vocabulary, practice pronunciation, develop their discussion skills, learn proverbs and songs, and gain familiarity with the contexts in which English is used. The text of each chapter matches the narration on the video.

Inside America is suitable for students in a listening-speaking class or an individualized lab. It is ideal for learners who are preparing for citizenship, employment, or further education in the United States. Because *Inside America* prompts the use of English in myriad settings, learners gain both skill and confidence in their ability to interact successfully with speakers of English in the United States.

I created *Inside America* in response to my students' request for more information about American culture. Many immigrants told me that they felt isolated in their ethnic communities. They wanted to learn the norms of American life while they improved their language skills. They recognized that commercial movies, television shows and soap operas do not reflect everyday reality, and they wanted to understand how typical Americans live. *Inside America* is the culmination of my effort to produce an honest picture of the United States.

I owe thanks to more students, colleagues, family and friends than I can possibly list here for their help and suggestions during the years it took to produce *Inside America*. However, I especially want to acknowledge Debra Barth; Todd Bruce; Jim Campbell; Angie Catalano;

Wayne Disher; Tom Entrikin; Virgil Frizzell; Anne Hickling; Jeff Kendall-Weed; Katie Kendall-Weed and friends; Henry Manayan; Pat McCrery; Amanda Morgan; Malika Mouwattakil; Margaret Muench; Andrea Santa Cruz; Bob Schleiker; Albert Solomon; Chui Tsang; Lynn, Ron and Michael Ward; Todd Williams.

Joe Weed produced the video and recorded the music, all of which he composed or arranged. Many of the instrumental selections are available on CD. For further information about the music, contact Highland Records at (800) 354-5580.

For comments or questions about *Inside America*, contact Highland Publishing at (408) 353-5756.

Martha E. Kendall
San Jose City College

1

Services to the Public

I. Get Ready

A. Before you watch the video, work with a partner to -

- list all the services offered to the public that you can think of.

- name at least two public services that you have used during the last twenty-four hours.

- name at least five jobs or careers that serve the public.

- pose a question you have about services to the public. If your question is not answered in the video, ask your teacher. Your teacher may tell you the answer, or refer you to an information source so you can get the answer yourself and share it with the class.

B. To improve your comprehension of the video, review this vocabulary:

smoke detector – a device that makes a loud warning sound if smoke is present

insurance - a purchased contract that promises money to the buyer if certain conditions occur, such as a health care cost

ticket - a written notice given by a police officer stating what was done wrong and the penalty

fine - money paid as a penalty for doing something wrong

violation – breaking a rule or law

bribe – money or a favor in exchange for special treatment

document - an official paper or certificate
misdemeanor – a minor crime
felony – a serious crime
defendant – a person accused of a crime
eligible – meeting certain requirements
donations - gifts or contributions
annual - yearly
volunteer – to work without getting paid

II.   Watch the Video

Watch and listen to the video. During the interview with Fire Captain Todd Bruce, notice his advice about how to be fire safe.

After watching the video, read the text below. It matches the narration.

Most American cities provide excellent fire protection. Some departments have an average response time of only four minutes between the emergency call and their arrival on the scene. Firefighters perform emergency rescues, and they educate the public about safety, such as the importance of having smoke detectors at home.

Ambulances carry ill or injured people who need immediate hospital care. Some hospitals provide health care to everyone, with government programs paying for low-income patients who do not have their own medical insurance.

Police protection helps maintain citizens' sense of security. Call 911 to report any emergency. Although the nickname for a police officer is a "cop," if you speak to a police officer, be polite. Call him or her "Officer."

The Department of Motor Vehicles issues driver's licenses to people over sixteen who pass a written test, vision test and road test. If you get a ticket, you will have to pay a fine. It is against the law to offer a bribe to try to avoid a ticket. If you believe you are not guilty of a violation, go to Traffic Court.

The U. S. Postal Service handles forty percent of the world's mail. Deliveries are made six days a week, Monday through Saturday, except for legal holidays.

At City Hall, do not hesitate to ask for information. There, you can apply for many official documents, such as a building permit, a business license, or a marriage license. To find out about legal services and government offices near you, check the phone book. If you call, you will probably hear a recorded message that you can listen to several times.

The Public Defender's office provides attorneys to poor people charged with a misdemeanor or felony. Defendants have the right to be represented by a lawyer even if they do not have the ability to pay.

Small Claims Court is available for cases that do not involve a criminal charge or a lot of money. There, you present your own case. Attorneys are not used.

The Department of Social Services offers many kinds of aid. Welfare money, health programs and food stamps are examples of help given to eligible low-income people.

Service agencies are struggling to deal with the increasing number of people living on America's streets. Many of the homeless are mentally ill or drug addicts.   Some of them are helped by charities such as the Salvation Army and Goodwill.   These agencies accept donations of food, used clothing and furniture. Among their many services, they provide job training to people with disabilities or other barriers to employment.

The YWCA, the Young Women's Christian Association, and the YMCA, the Young Men's Christian Association, are national organizations open to people of any religion. Nicknamed simply the "Y," they provide a range of reasonably-priced activities such as fitness programs, swim lessons, and summer camps for children.

The Chamber of Commerce promotes business in the community. The Tourist and Convention Bureau gives free information about nearby places of interest and special things to see and do.

Americans consume more than do citizens of any other country. Many cities sponsor recycling programs. It's important to recycle cans, bottles, plastic and paper.

At the public library, you can borrow books, videos, CDs and magazines at no cost. The library offers a quiet place to read, relax, or search for information on a computer. Before the annual income tax deadline on April 15, many libraries offer help in completing tax forms.

Free education is probably the most valuable service in America.

Children begin kindergarten at age five. After completing six years of elementary school, they attend a middle school. Must students complete high school when they are about eighteen years old. People who have not finished high school may learn basic skills at an adult education program.

At low-cost community colleges, students may enroll in just a few classes or complete the first two years of university study. Public colleges and universities offer the least expensive higher education.

State agencies such as the Employment Development Department help people find jobs. But there's more to life than work! Most cities have a Parks and Recreation Department that organizes sports activities, provides recreation for children, and maintains zoos, community centers, public parks and pools. Senior centers provide social and recreational programs for older citizens. Many cities have civic auditoriums, art galleries and museums.

Of course, services are of little use if you can't get to them. Trains, buses, planes, bikes and cars make Americans the most mobile people in the world.

Almost every city has volunteer service organizations such as the Rotary Club and the Lions Club. By working together, private citizens and public agencies help all Americans enjoy healthier, happier lives.

III. Understand It

A. Enlarging your vocabulary improves your comprehension. Each unit contains a different activity for learning vocabulary. Try each way at least once. As you study new words, repeat the activities that work best for you.

Write each word on a slip of paper or 3 x 5 card. Write each definition on one, too. Turn all the cards over and distribute them on a flat surface. Now play the memory game in which two or three players take turns flipping over any two cards and reading them aloud. If the chosen cards contain a word and its definition, then that player has made a match, will collect the two cards, and take another turn. If the cards do not match, they are both turned back over, replaced in the same spot, and the next player takes a turn. When all the cards have been matched and picked up, the winner is the person who has the most cards.

B. With a partner, take turns asking these questions and answering them in complete sentences.

1. What does the fire department encourage people to have in their homes?
2. What are ambulances for?
3. How can you report an emergency?
4. What is the polite name for a "cop"?
5. Where can you get a driver's license?
6. What should you do if you believe you are not guilty of a violation?
7. Where can you get a business or marriage license?
8. What does the Public Defender's office do?
9. What kinds of cases are presented at Small Claims Court?
10. What are some examples of aid offered by the Department of Social Services?
11. What are two examples of charities?
12. What do the YMCA and the YWCA do?
13. What does the Chamber of Commerce do?
14. What does the Tourist and Convention Bureau do?
15. What should be recycled?
16. What can you borrow from the public library?
17. Where can adults learn basic skills?
18. Which colleges and universities are least expensive?
19. What state agency helps people find jobs?
20. What does the Parks and Recreation Department do?

IV. Practice It

A. Fill in the blanks with a word or phrase.

1. Fire departments educate the public about the importance of

having a smoke _____.

2. Call _____ to report an emergency.

3. People over sixteen who pass a written test, vision test and road

test may get a _____.

4. A person who receives a ticket must pay a_____.

5. At _____, attorneys are not used.

6. Welfare money, health programs and food stamps are examples of

help to given to eligible _____people.

7. _____organize activities for older people.

8. The _____ helps people find jobs.

9. The _____ offers free

information about places of interest in the city.

10. People who have not graduated from high school may learn basic

skills at an _____program.

B. Working with a partner, take turns asking the following questions about your city. Answer in a word or phrase.

1. Quick! How can I report an emergency?
2. Where can I apply for a driver's license?
3. I've been charged with a crime, but I can't afford an attorney. Where should I go for help?
4. A dishonest mechanic failed to fix my car, but he refuses to give me my money back. What can I do?
5. My family needs money and food until we can find jobs here.

Where can we go for help?

6. I'm too old for high school, but I still need to learn many basic skills. Where can I go to school?
7. Where can I find out about places of interest to visit in this city?
8. Where can I get help finding a job?
9. My girlfriend and I want to get married. Where can we get a marriage license?
10. Where can I find out about children's programs in public parks?

V. Say It Well

A. Sentences have different meanings depending on which word is stressed. The stressed words in the sentences below are printed in **bold**. The stressed syllables are also underlined.

- Where are you going in the **fall**?

> I'm going to **college** in the fall.

- **When** are you going to college?

> I'm going to college in the **fall**.

With a partner, take turns practicing these dialogs. Emphasize the stressed syllables of the words printed in bold by saying them louder, higher and slower.

1. Have you got your **license** yet?

> I got it last **month**.

When are you getting **married**?

> I'm **not** getting married!

What's the **license** for?

> It's for driving a **car**!

Aren't you ever getting **married**?

> That **depends**.

Depends on **what**?

> Will **you** marry me?

I will if you get a **marriage** license!

2. Does the library handle **e<u>mer</u>gencies**?

                  No, the **pol<u>ice</u>** do.

What **<u>does</u>** the library do?

                  It loans **books**.

3. What is the **Chamber of <u>Com</u>merce**?

                  It's an **organi<u>za</u>tion**.

What does it **<u>do</u>**?

                  It promotes **business**.

B. Make up your own dialogs. Follow this pattern, stressing words from this unit as much as you can:

1. Did you **volun<u>teer</u>**?

             No, I was **paid**.

2. Is that the **DM<u>V</u>**?

             No, it's the **EDD**.

3. Is that the **pol<u>ice</u>** department?

             No, it's the **<u>fire</u>** department.

4. _____

      _____

5. _____

      _____

6. _____

      _____

VI. Discuss It

Think about the following ideas so that you'll be prepared to talk about them in class.

1. For most immigrants, improving their fluency in English makes them more self-sufficient. List specific benefits you expect to gain as a result of improving your English.

2. Drug abuse is a major social problem in the United States. Do you think drugs should be made legal so that users are not criminals? Is drug abuse a problem in your native country?

3. Is it common for children in your native country to want to become firefighters when they grow up? When you were a child, what did you want to be? Now, what do you want in your future?

4. Compare driving a car in the United States with driving in your native country.

5. Do you think people on welfare become dependent and lazy? Should there be a limit on how long a person can collect welfare money?

6. Act out the situations described below. The class members who do not volunteer to play roles will vote to decide which character can use the taxi cab. Before making their decision, they may ask the characters to answer questions. The characters may create stories to improve their chances of "winning" the ride in the taxi cab. Have fun!

The scene: one taxi cab driver, surrounded by three excited people. Each person wants to hire the cab. The driver can not decide which person to take.
Tuan Tran: He wants to get to his college class.
Mary Martinez: She wants to get her medicine at the drug store.
John Jones: He wants to see his girlfriend who is waiting for him.

Repeat the scene, this time using these three characters:
Ann Wong: She has an appointment at the EDD with a counselor who will help her find a job.
Carlos Perez: His car broke down, and he needs to get to work.
Tanya Washington: She wants to take her driver's tests at the DMV.

7. Years ago, few government programs helped new immigrants in the United States. Today, many social services agencies paid for by American taxpayers provide help for them. Some people who came during the old days say, "I made it on my own. New immigrants today should, too." What do you think?

8. Research a well-known trial, read about a current legal case, or make up a situation in which a defendant is accused of a crime. State the facts of the case, and then ask for volunteers to act as judge, lawyers, witnesses, and the defendant in a trial. They can add information as they act out their roles. The rest of the class will be the jury, voting to determine the defendant's innocence or guilt.

VII. Explore the Community

The best way to learn English is to use it. Doing these activities will give you lots of practice in English.

To find the addresses of most of the places listed below, look in your phone book. Call the offices to check the hours they are open.

When you visit any of these offices, you may be given written information. Bring it with you to show the class. Also, be prepared to explain to the class what you did and what you found out.

1. If you do not already have a driver's license, go to the Department of Motor Vehicles and find out about regulations for getting one. Read what you are given, and ask questions if it isn't clear.

2. Contact the Department of Motor Vehicles to find out where and when Traffic Court is in session. Go watch what happens there.

3. Contact the County Clerk, City Hall, or you local courthouse to find out where and when Small Claims Court is in session. Go watch what happens there.

4. If you do not already have a library card, go to your public library and apply for one.

5.   Get information about programs offered at the YMCA or YWCA.

6.   Go to the Social Services Department and get information about programs offered there.

7.   Go to the Chamber of Commerce or the Tourist and Convention Bureau and get information about your city.

8.   Go to a public hospital and find out what a person must do to be admitted for emergency care.

9.   Visit a senior center and find out about its programs and services.

10.   Go to the state employment development department and find out what help is offered to people looking for work.

11.   Visit a recycling center. Find out what can be recycled, what the hours are, and if any money is given for recycled materials.

12.   Visit a museum or art gallery.

13.   Go to the Public Defender's office and get information about their services and who is eligible for them.

14.   Find out what the Parks and Recreation Department offers.

15.   Visit a charitable agency such as Hospice, Goodwill, Catholic Charities or the Red Cross. Find out what services are provided, and whether there's a need for volunteers.

16.   Find out if your community has a battered women's shelter and what services it provides for abused women and their children.

17.   Find out how your community helps homeless people.

18.   Look in the yellow pages of your phone book to find an agency or company that offers a service that interests you. Imagine that agency or company has hired you to make their recorded phone message. To hear examples of messages, call a bus company, a bank, the Department of Motor Vehicles or the Immigration and Naturalization Service. Use

your tape recorder to create an original, appropriate message for the company or agency that "hired" you. You may want to include a menu of options. Play your complete message for the class.

VIII.   Debate It

Form debate teams that argue *pro (yes)* or *con (no)* on the following topics. After listening to the teams' arguments, students in the rest of the class may ask questions of the teams, and then vote *pro* or *con* in secret ballot.

1. All residents of the United States deserve free health care, regardless of the cost.

2. Low-income parents on welfare deserve additional money from the government whenever a baby is added to the family.

3. All children should be allowed to attend free public schools, even if their parents entered the United States illegally.

4. Debate a topic you choose that relates to this unit. State the idea in one sentence so that people can argue *pro* or *con*.

IX.   Consider the Proverbs

Guess what each of these sayings means. Then, give an example that illustrates each one. Be prepared to share it with the class. Does your native language have any of the same proverbs? If so, compare them.

1.   The early bird gets the worm.
2.   Waste not, want not.
3.   When it rains, it pours.
4.   A friend in need is a friend indeed.
5.   Do unto others as you would have others do unto you.

2
American Government

I. Get Ready

A. Before you watch the video, work with a partner to -

- name at least three people in American government.

- imagine that a child has asked you to explain American government. What single most important idea would you include in your answer, and why?

- pose a question you have about American government. If your question is not answered in the video, ask your teacher. Your teacher may tell you the answer, or refer you to an information source so you can get the answer yourself and share it with the class.

B. To improve your comprehension of the video, review this vocabulary:

legislative - law-making
executive - administering the law
administrator - a person in charge of a bureaucracy
judicial - relating to judges and courts
implementation- making something happen
U.S. Constitution - the document defining American government
governor - a head of state government
mayor - a head of city government
fundamental - basic
democracy - a system of government elected by the people

campaign - a candidates' efforts to win an election
candidate for office - a person who wants to be elected
controversial - debatable; lacking agreement
ballot - a list of candidates and issues to be voted on
polls - where people vote

II. Watch the Video

Watch and listen to the video. During the interview with Henry Manayan, Mayor of Milpitas, California, notice his encouragement to participate in American democracy.

After watching the video, read the text below. It matches the narration.

Washington, D.C. is the capital of the United States. The government is organized into three main branches, a system that creates a balance in power.

The legislative branch, called the Congress, makes the laws. This branch is divided into two parts. The Senate consists of one hundred Senators, two from each state. They are elected for six-year terms. The House of Representatives has almost 450 members, each elected for a two-year term. Representation is based on population. Therefore, the states with the most people have the most Representatives in the House.

The executive branch is led by the President and Vice President, elected for four-year terms. The President lives in the White House and works in the oval office. If the legislative branch passes a bill, it becomes law after the President signs it. As chief administrator, the President appoints a Cabinet, including the Secretary of State, Secretary of Defense and the Secretary of the Interior.

The judicial branch judges the implementation of the laws and whether or not they meet the standards of the United States Constitution. Additions and changes to the Constitution are called amendments. The first ten amendments, nicknamed the Bill of Rights, guarantee basic freedoms such as freedom of speech, the press and religion.

Many states' governments are similar, with their own executive, legislative and judicial branches. Each state has its own governor, and most cities elect a mayor.

Certainly one of the most fundamental rights in our democracy is the right to vote. You know an election is coming when you see the many campaign signs put up by candidates for office. A good citizen needs to stay informed about current political issues in order to make wise choices.

Any citizen over eighteen is free either to join a party or remain independent. The Democratic and Republican parties are the biggest. In the primary election in the spring, each party chooses its candidates. The winning candidates compete for votes in the general election, held in early November.

In order to vote, you must be a United States citizen at least eighteen years old. To register, simply fill out a short form, available at many government offices. After registering, you will be sent a sample ballot so you can study the candidates and issues before election day. Translating the ballot into other languages besides English has become controversial, because some people want English to be the only official language in the United States.

At the polls on election day, you will be asked to sign your name. If you have any questions about how to vote, you may ask to use a sample machine. Then you will vote in private, casting a secret ballot. Sometimes as many as half the eligible citizens do not vote in an election. Some of them say that one vote does not make a difference.

American democracy was designed to be "of the people, by the people and for the people." It is people who make a country great.

III. Understand It

A. Enlarging your vocabulary improves your comprehension. Each unit contains a different activity for learning vocabulary. Try each way at least once. As you study new words, repeat the activities that work best for you.

Cut two small slips of paper. On one, write a vocabulary word. On the other, write its meaning. Put all the students' slips in a basket and mix them up. Then, have each person draw two slips. When the teacher gives the signal, everybody gets up and starts talking and exchanging slips with classmates. The game is over when everyone has a pair of slips with a vocabulary word and its correct meaning.

B. With a partner, take turns asking these questions and answering them in complete sentences.

1.   What are the three main branches of American government?
2.   What does the Congress do?
3.   What are the two parts of the Congress?
4.   How many Senators are in the U. S. Senate?
5.   How long is a Senator's term of office?
6.   How long is a Representative's term of office?
7.   Who leads the executive branch?
8.   How long is a President's term of office?
9.   Where does the President work?
10.   When does a bill become law?
11.   Who appoints the Cabinet?
12.   What does the judicial branch do?
13.   What are amendments?
14.   What is the Bill of Rights?
15.   Which parties are the biggest?
16.   What is an advantage in joining a party?
17.   When is the general election?
18.   Who can vote?
19.   Where can you get a voter registration form?
20.   What is each registered voter sent before the election?

IV. Apply It

A. Fill in the blanks using the words in the list provided. They will not all be used.

legislative	controversial
executive	administrator
judicial	ballots

polls   governor
mayor   campaign
U.S. Constitution   democracy

When candidates run a _____ to win an

election, they try to convince voters to cast their

_____ for them at the _____. They

may debate_____ issues with other candidates.

According to the _____, American

citizens elect their own leaders.   This system is called a

_____.

Sometimes the leader of a state, called a _____,

first gains political experience as a_____ leading

a city.   Both positions are part of the _____ branch

of government.

B. Fill in each blank, giving the name of the person who now holds each office listed. You can find the information in your library.

1. President of the United States:_____

2. Vice President of the United States:_____

3. Secretary of State: _____

4. Secretary of Defense:_____

5. Secretary of the Interior:_____

6. Chief Justice of the U. S. Supreme Court:_____

7. The two U.S. Senators for your state:_____

   and_____

8. The U. S. Representative for your district:_____

9. The Governor of your state:_____

10. The Mayor of your city:_____

V. Agree or Disagree

A fundamental part of democracy is people's freedom to state opinions that agree or disagree.

One way of agreeing is to emphasize the verb by saying it higher, longer and louder. One way of disagreeing is to emphasize **I**. Working with a partner, practice these patterns. Stress the underlined syllable in bold.   Then make up your own dialogs, following this pattern to express agreement and disagreement.

1. "He is a good President."
                   "Yes, he **is**."   or   "**I** don't think so."

2. "She speaks very effectively."
                   "Yes, she **does**."   or   "**I** don't think so."

3. "They make good decisions."
                   "Yes, they **do**."   or   "**I** don't think so."

4. _____

   _____ or _____

5. _____

_____ or _____

6. _____

_____ or _____

VI. Discuss It

Think about the following ideas so that you'll be prepared to talk about them in class.

1.   Compare the national government of your native country with American government.

2.   American citizens at least eighteen years old are eligible to vote. Do you think the voting age should be changed?

3.   "It's a free country," Americans often say. Explain what freedom means to you.

4.   America is said to be the land of equal opportunity for all. Do you think this describes the United States today? Give specific examples.

5.   Do you think a woman could win an election for U.S. President today? Why or why not?

6.   Form groups of three or four students. Imagine that the President has invited your group to come talk to him about the issues of greatest concern to you. Make a list of topics you will discuss with him. Explain to the whole class what your group will tell the President.

7.   If you could be the President of the United States for a day, what would you do during your twenty-four hours on the job?

8.   Discuss any current political issue of interest to the class.

VII. Use It

The best way to learn English is to use it. Doing these activities will give you lots of practice in English.

The easiest way to find most of the places listed below is by looking in your phone book.

When you visit the offices, you may be given written information. Bring it with you to show the class. Also, be prepared to explain what you did and what you found out.

1.   Visit your local Democratic and Republican Party offices. Ask for information about each party. Contrast their principles, using their views on two or three current political issues to show some of the differences.

2.   Research the history of the Republican or Democratic party.

3.   Get information about any of the smaller political parties, such as the American Independent Party, the Party for Peace and Freedom, the Green Party, the Libertarian Party, etc.

4.   Volunteer to work at the offices of a political party, or for a candidate running for office.

5.   Get a voter registration form from City Hall, the Post Office or Fire Department. Find out if it is available in other languages, and if so, which ones.

6.   Find out the steps required to become a U.S. citizen by contacting the Immigration and Naturalization Service.

7.   Write a short letter explaining your opinion on a current political issue. Send copies to your U.S. Senator, your U.S. Representative and the President. Compare the replies you receive. In class, summarize your letter and the replies.

8.   Visit your state capitol building, or the office of your Mayor, U.S. Senator or Representative, or state legislators. Find out what the

elected officials do, and what services they provide.

9.   Study the Bill of Rights, and briefly explain the meaning of each one.

10.   Choose a current political issue or news event, and compare stories about it in two different newspapers, magazines or TV broadcasts.

11.   Begin every class period with a student's summary of a current news event that relates to the government, and allow time for a brief discussion about it.

12.   Check to see if your library has a video of any Presidential debates. Watch the debates, summarize the candidates' views, and explain why you favor one or the other.

13.   Stage an election in your class. Decide what offices are to be voted on, possibly mayor of your city, president of the students' association, president of the U.S., etc. Have students volunteer to be candidates and give speeches about why the rest of the class should vote for them. Using secret ballots, hold your election.

16.   The foreign-born account for almost ten percent of the U.S. population. What percent of your state's population is foreign-born? Research immigrants' impact on your state's economy, schools, health care, etc. Do you think the federal government should limit further immigration?

17.   Find out what kinds of people generally are elected to government offices. Choose one or two positions, such as City Council Member, Mayor, Governor, Senator, or President. For the position(s) you're researching, do you find any patterns in the age, sex, race, income level, education or profession of people in office?

18.   Research the history of the American national anthem, *The Star-Spangled Banner*. The music is in the Appendix.

VIII.   Debate It

Form debate teams that argue *pro* or *con* on the following topics. After listening to the teams' arguments, students in the rest of the class may ask questions of the teams, and then vote *pro* or *con* in secret ballot.

1. English should be the official language of the United States, and government information should be printed in English only.

2. Citizens should have the right to own handguns.

3. This amendment should be added to the Unites States Constitution: "A citizen's rights shall not be abridged or denied on account of sex."

4. Debate a topic you choose that relates to this unit. State the idea in one sentence so that people can argue *pro* or *con*.

IX.   Consider the Proverbs

Guess what each of these sayings means. Then, give an example that illustrates each one. Be prepared to share it with the class. Does your native language have any of the same proverbs? If so, compare them.

1. A stitch in time saves nine.
2. Save for a rainy day.
3. The squeaky wheel gets the grease.
4. Live and let live.
5. Those who hesitate are lost.

3

Growing Up in America

I. Get Ready

A. Before you watch the video, work with a partner to -

- describe what you have observed about the daily lives of American children.

- describe the life of an American child shown on TV or in a movie.

- pose a question you have about growing up in America. If your question is not answered in the video, ask your teacher. Your teacher may tell you the answer, or refer you to an information source so you can get the answer yourself and share it with the class.

B. To improve your comprehension of the video, review this vocabulary:

pregnant - expecting a baby
infant - a baby
prenatal - before the birth
chores - small jobs

controversy - a disagreement
upbringing - childhood
immunized - vaccinated to prevent disease
toddler - a small child who has just learned to walk
miniature - very small
slumber - sleeping
allowance - a small amount of money for routine expenses
annual - yearly
fund-raiser - an event to earn money for a charitable cause
illegal - against the law
reception - a party in honor of someone, often a bride and groom
anniversary - a yearly celebration

II. Watch the Video

Watch and listen to the video. During the interview with Angie Catalano, notice her encouragement to make the most of opportunities in school, at work and in sports.

After watching the video, read the text below. It matches the narration.

A baby shower is a party for a woman about to become a mother. Friends give her clothes, toys and furniture for the new baby. Happy and excited, the pregnant woman looks forward to the baby's arrival. She and her husband may take classes to learn about child birth and infant care.   Prenatal medical care helps insure the development of a healthy baby.

At the hospital, the new father takes an active role during and after the baby's birth. The mother and baby usually stay in the hospital for a day or two. At home, mothers and fathers both take part in infant care. In many families, the husband and wife also share the household chores.

Today, most American families have only one or two children. The recent increase in the number of single, teenage mothers has caused a controversy about whether children can have a happy, healthy upbringing in a single-parent home.

One important responsibility for parents is to have their babies immunized against disease. Another safety issue is that any guns in the home must be locked up.

Older brothers and sisters may help care for younger children. Grandparents sometimes babysit as well. For many youngsters, the family dog makes an understanding friend. Toddlers love to try everything, from making cookies to pretending to drive. Of course, children must be buckled into their seat belts whenever they ride in a car.

Many kids go to nursery school or a day-care center while their parents are at school or work. They make new friends and learn new things, like how to climb a tree or ride a tricycle.

At a birthday party, the kids wear party hats. The birthday girl cuts the cake, and her friends give her presents. The number of candles on the birthday cake matches her age. If she blows out all the candles in one breath, then her secret wish will come true.

At a fair, kids may play follow-the-leader with a clown, ride on a merry-go-round, play miniature golf or ride the roller coaster. Don't forget the camera!

The most popular team sports for children are soccer, basketball and baseball. Many kids like to ride bikes, roller blade, play roller hockey, skate board and hang out with friends. On sunny days, youngsters may go to a park to enjoy the swing, go down the slide, play catch, fly a kite, play with friends, or have a picnic with the family. In the summer, what could be better than buying ice cream, swimming in a pool, playing at the beach, feeding the ducks, going hiking or fishing?

For indoor fun, many kids practice karate, go to the arcade, or eat pizza with friends. At home, they may watch TV, play games, hug the cat, use the computer, or play an instrument. Many kids like to invite friends to spend the night at their house for a slumber party.

Most parents give their kids a weekly allowance. To earn extra money, some teenagers get a paper route and deliver newspapers before or after school. Maybe some of the money will be spent to pay for a hair cut, new clothes, or just an ice cream cone.

Kids should have their teeth cleaned and examined by a dentist at least twice a year. Many children need to have their teeth straightened by the orthodontist. Kids must also see the doctor for regular check-ups and keep their immunizations current.

Although Christianity is not the only religion in the United States, it is the most common.

The Girl Scouts and the Boy Scouts are national organizations many kids choose to join. Scouts often do service projects in the community, such as raking leaves from a church parking lot. You may be asked to buy cookies at the annual fund-raiser for Girl Scouts, the cookie sale.

Teenagers like to spend time with friends and play sports. Many have part-time and summer jobs, often at fast-food restaurants. Unfortunately, some teens use illegal drugs, a problem that has become a major social concern.

An important part of life for young men and women is going on dates. They may share lunch, go out for dinner, or just enjoy time together. Most Americans get married. The wedding ceremony is followed by a reception where the bride and groom cut the wedding cake. About half of the first marriages in the United States end in divorce, but second marriages are common. Naturally, everyone hopes their marriage will succeed, and they will celebrate many happy anniversaries.

III. Understand It

A. Enlarging your vocabulary improves your comprehension. Each unit contains a different activity for learning vocabulary. Try each way at least once. As you study new words, repeat the activities that work best for you.

Play the game called "charades." Choose a word from the vocabulary list and silently act it out. Classmates try to guess which word you are dramatizing.

B. With a partner, take turns asking these questions and answering them in complete sentences.

1. What is a baby shower?
2. What classes might a pregnant woman take?
3. What helps a baby develop good health?
4. Who takes care of the infant?
5. How many children do most American families have?

6. What are two important responsibilities for parents?
7. How must children ride in a car?
8. What happens at a birthday party?
9. What do the candles on a birthday cake show?
10. What might children do at a fair?
11. What are the most popular team sports?
12. What are some other sports kids enjoy?
13. What can kids do at the park?
14. What are some common activities at home?
15. How do some kids earn extra money?
16. How often should children see the dentist?
17. What are the Girl Scouts and Boy Scouts of America?
18. Where do many teenagers find part-time or summer jobs?
19. What usually follows the church wedding ceremony?
20. How many American first marriages end in divorce?

C. Working with a partner, write the letter of the definition that best fits each word.

1._____ anniversary   A. event that earns money

2. _____chores   B. childhood

3. _____immunized   C. baby

4. _____toddler   D. protected from disease

5. _____fund-raiser   E. small child

6. _____allowance   F. money

7. _____reception   G. yearly celebration

8. _____ infant   H. sleep

9. _____upbringing   I. party

10._____slumber   J. small jobs

IV. Practice the Prefixes

Prefixes are syllables added to the beginning of a word. Learning ten common prefixes can significantly increase your vocabulary because the prefixes occur in hundreds of words. Working with a partner, give at least two more examples of words using the following prefixes:

1. pre = before
"Prenatal" means "before the birth."
"Preview" means "before the regular opportunity for viewing."
Give two more examples beginning with "pre" —

_____ means _____

_____ means _____

2. re = again
"Rewind" means "wind again."
"Review" means "look again."
Give two more examples beginning with "re" —

_____ means _____

_____ means _____

3. bi = two
"Bicycle" means "two wheels."
"Biweekly" means "every two weeks."
Give two more examples beginning with "bi" —

_____ means _____

_____ means _____

4. sub = below, under
"Substandard" means "below the normal."
"Submarine" means "below the water."

Give two more examples beginning with "sub" —

_____ means _____

_____ means _____

5. *super = above*
"Superior" means "above all others."
"Supervisor" means "leader."
Give two more examples beginning with "super" —

_____ means _____

_____ means _____

6. *de = removed or lessened*
"Demote" means to "move to a lower job."
"Decrease" means to "make smaller."
Give two more examples beginning with "de" —

_____ means _____

_____ means _____

7. *auto = self*
"Automobile" means "vehicle that moves by itself."
"Autobiography" is the "story of your own life."
Give two more examples beginning with "auto" —

_____ means _____

_____ means _____

8. *inter = between*
"Internet" refers to "communication between computers."
"International" means "between nations."
Give two more examples beginning with "inter" —

_____ means _____

_____ means _____

9. *un = not* or *the reversal of an action*
"Unfriendly" means "not friendly."
"Unleash" means "to remove from a leash."
Give two more examples beginning with "un" —

_____ means _____

_____ means _____

10. *con = with, together*
"Consecutive" means "at the same time."
"Converge" means "to join together."
Give two more examples beginning with "con" —

_____ means _____

_____ means _____

Add the appropriate prefix to the following word roots. Several will be used more than once.

1. _____ requisite (required in advance)

2. _____ merit (loss of points)

3. _____ test (an exam taken before other activities)

4. _____ partisan (both parties)

5. _____ ordinate (below another person's authority)

6. _____ new (get again)

7. _____ let (rented under someone's lease)

8. _____ focals (having two lenses)

9. _____ vise (check again)

10. _____ value (become less in worth)

11. _____ lative (best)

12._____ nomy (in charge of yourself)

13. _____ continental (between continents)

14. _____ likely (not)

15. _____ current (at the same time)

V. Discuss It

Think about the following ideas so that you'll be prepared to talk about them in class.

1. Many Americans believe that children spend too much time watching television. What are some benefits of watching television? What are some disadvantages? Should parents limit the amount of time their children watch TV?

2. Many parents leave their children at day-care centers while they go to work. Some people say this is not good for the children. They say kids need parental attention all day long. What do you think?

3. Although most Americans get married, it has become common for young couples to live together for several months or years before they legally marry. Do you think this is a good idea?

4. What are the qualities of a good parent? List at least ten adjectives describing an ideal mother or father. Do you think these are the same for parents in all cultures?

5. Children learn to express their emotions in ways that are acceptable in the culture in which they are growing up. People who grew up in different cultures may express the same emotion quite differently. In groups, describe the appropriate way men, women and children in your native country express the emotions listed below. In general, how do most Americans express them?

- happiness
- sadness
- worry
- reverence

- confidence
- humility
- anger
- pain

- love
- embarrassment
- impatience
- fear

6. Discuss how one of the topics listed relates to your native culture. (More than one student may talk about each topic, as long as different countries are being described. This will prevent repetition. Or, students may organize panel discussions so that several people contribute to the explanation of each topic.)

A.   courtship and dating

B.   wedding ceremony

C.   wedding reception

D.   attitude toward divorce

E.   attitude toward number of children

F.   naming of children

G.   birthday celebrations

H.   childbirth

I.   treatment of the elderly

J.   funerals

K.   _?_ (Your own topic that relates to this unit)

VI. Use It

The best way to learn English is to use it. Doing these activities will give you lots of practice in English. Be prepared to explain to the class what you did.

1.   If it is allowed, visit the maternity ward of your local hospital. Get information about health care during pregnancy and delivery.

2.   Spend an afternoon watching or helping at a nursery school or day-care center.

3.   Attend a meeting of the Girl Scouts or the Boy Scouts. You can probably contact a Scout leader through an elementary school.

4.   Attend a fair, festival or circus, and tell the class what you saw and did there.

5.   Watch a sporting event for children or teenagers, such as Little League baseball, a swim meet, a football or basketball game.

6.   Ask American children of different ages what they expect to be when they grow up. Compare their answers with the typical choices made by children in your native country.

7.   Traditionally, when women in the United States get married, they drop their original last name and use their husband's. The baby is also given the husband's last name. For the baby's first and middle names, some parents name the baby after a relative or friend, or they may simply choose names they like. Ask at least five Americans how they were named, or how they named their children.

8.   In groups, prepare a brief questionnaire for parents. On it, list at least eight qualities that you think parents would like their children to have, such as independence, obedience, humility, etc. Ask several American parents to select from your list the two traits they consider most important. Share your findings with the class. Do you think parents in your native country would want the same traits in their children? Is there a difference in traits desired for girls and boys?

9. Visit a pet store or a humane society. Find out which pets would be good for a family with small children.

10. Lead the class in singing *Make New Friends* and *Happy Birthday*. The music is provided in the Appendix.

VII. Debate It

Form debate teams that argue *pro* or *con* on the following topics. After listening to the teams' arguments, students in the rest of the class may ask questions of the teams, and then vote *pro* or *con* in secret ballot.

1. To reduce the divorce rate, couples should be required to wait at least two years to marry after they apply for their marriage license.

2. A couple and the baby they adopt should be of the same race.

3. Abortion should be legal.

4. Debate a topic you choose that relates to this unit. State the idea in one sentence so that people can argue pro or con.

VIII. Consider the Proverbs

Guess what each of these sayings means. Then, give an example that illustrates each one. Be prepared to share it with the class. Does your native language have any of the same proverbs? If so, compare them.

1. Don't count your chickens before they've hatched.
2. It takes a village to raise a child.
3. Youth is wasted on the young.
4. An apple a day keeps the doctor away.
5. Don't put the cart before the horse.

4

The School System

I. Get Ready

A. Before you watch the video, work with a partner to -

- list as many subjects taught in school as you can.

- name as many schools as you can.

- write your educational goals.

- pose a question you have about American schools. If your question is not answered in the video, ask your teacher. Your teacher may tell you the answer, or refer you to an information source so you can get the answer yourself and share it with the class.

B. To improve your comprehension of the video, review this vocabulary:

cooperate - to work well (with other people)
ABC's - the alphabet
academic - relating to school
tuition - money paid to attend school
enroll - to sign up for
private - not open to everyone
parochial - religious
bilingual - able to speak two languages
extracurricular - in addition to the regular school subjects
memorable - worth remembering

equivalent - same
affordable - not too expensive
scholarship - money given to a qualified student

II. Watch the Video

Watch and listen to the video. During the interview with San Jose City College President Chui Tsang, notice his encouragement to practice English as much as you can while you are in school.

After watching the video, read the text below. It matches the narration.

Many parents pay for their children to attend preschool when they are three or four years old. The children learn how to cooperate with others. They may also learn their ABC's.

Most children begin kindergarten at age five. Although a few schools use a year-round calendar, the traditional academic year lasts from September through June.

Most kids attend a free public school, but some parents pay tuition and enroll their children in a private or parochial school. A few parents educate their children themselves in independent home study. The key to children's academic success is how much interest their parents show in their education.

At age six, children enter first grade. Elementary school usually includes kindergarten through grades five or six. Students may walk to school, take the bus, ride a bike, or drive with their parents. They study many subjects, but the basics are nicknamed the "three R's" for reading, writing and arithmetic. Kids are also taught the dangers of drug use.

Bilingual education is sometimes available for students who do not speak English. Many schools teach children about the variety of cultural heritages reflected in America today.

Teachers call children by their first names. To show respect, children use their teacher's last name, such as Ms. Jones or Mr. Smith.

Education includes more than just academics. Students participate in plays and shows, which their proud parents may videotape. Kids gather for assemblies, play sports, and learn to get along on the playground. Sometimes classes take a field trip to visit a special place, like a museum or the fire station.

About age eleven, children graduate from elementary school and enter middle school or junior high, which is usually grades six, seven and eight.

High school includes grades nine through twelve: the freshman, sophomore, junior and senior years. Quite a bit of studying and homework are required, but most students find time for extracurricular activities and sports. Football games are popular for players and cheerleaders. Musicians march in the band. The prom, a formal dance, offers a chance for teenagers to get dressed up for a memorable night.

By law, all American children must attend school until they are at least sixteen years old. If they drop out before graduating from high school, they may later take adult education classes to earn the equivalent of a high school diploma. Most teenagers graduate from high school, and many go on to college.

The most affordable higher education is usually at a community college. Students can earn an Associate's degree after two years of full-time study, but many students attend part-time. Some get jobs on campus in work/study programs. College students meet new people, study hard, and they may play sports.

The four years of college have the same names as the four years in high school: freshman, sophomore, junior, senior. After graduating from a community college, students may transfer as a junior to a four-year college or university. Or, instead of attending community college for the first two years, a high school graduate may choose to enroll directly in a four-year college to earn a Bachelor's degree. Tuition is lower at a state college than at a private school. Well-qualified students may be eligible for a scholarship.

The difference between a college and a university is that the most advanced degree a college offers is an Associate's or Bachelor's. At a university, students may continue beyond the Bachelor's to get a Master's (M.A.) or a Doctorate (Ph.D.). Earning a Bachelor's makes someone a "college graduate," regardless of whether the degree is from a college or university.

In the United States, students of all ages come to college. Because of the changing workplace, many people return to school to update their skills or prepare for a new career. Immigrants who speak English well can expect to earn, on average, more than twice as much as workers who do not speak English. It's never too late to learn and earn more.

III. Understand It

A. Enlarging your vocabulary improves your comprehension. Each unit contains a different activity for learning vocabulary. Try each way at least once. As you study new words, repeat the activities that work best for you.

Play the "scramble" game. Working in teams of two or three people, select three words from the vocabulary list. For each word, write the letters it contains, but not in correct order. Spell the word so that it can be pronounced. For example, the word "museum" might be scrambled as "usemum." After all the teams have jumbled their three words, exchange the scrambled words with those written by other teams. Then, starting at the same time, all the teams begin to unscramble the words as quickly as possible. The first team to straighten out their words "wins."

After each team has written their words correctly, they should compose three sentences, using one of the vocabulary words in each. Write the sentences on the board, but leave a blank where the vocabulary word fits. Members of other teams fill in the blanks.

B. With a partner, take turns asking these questions and answering them in complete sentences.

1. At what age are children required to start school?
2. What is the first year of school called?
3. When is the traditional academic year?
4. Which school is free?
5. Which schools charge tuition?
6. What grades are in elementary school?
7. What are the three "R's"?
8. What service is sometimes available for children who do not speak English?
9. What names do teachers use for the children?

10. What names do children use for their teachers?
11. Where do some children go on field trips?
12. What grades are usually in middle school?
13. What are the names for the four years in high school or college?
14. What is the prom?
15. Until what age must children attend school?
16. What is the most affordable college for an A.A. degree?
17. How many years of full-time study are required for an A.A. degree?
18. Where can a student earn a Bachelor's degree?
19. What is the most affordable college for a Bachelor's?
20. Where can a student earn a Master's degree or Doctorate?

IV. Practice It

A. Write the letter of the word or phase from the list on the right which best matches the word from the list on the left.

_____1. sophomore

A. last year of high school

_____2. public

B. third year of high school

_____3. parochial

C. second year of high school

_____4. 3 R's

D. open for anyone

_____5. junior

E. first year of high school

_____6. kindergarten

F. reading, writing, arithmetic

_____7. freshman

G. money paid to attend school

_____8. extracurricular

H. activities in addition to studies

_____9. senior

I. first year of school

_____10. tuition

J. religious

B. Fill in the blanks with the words in the list below. Each will be used once.

parochial	bilingual
tuition	private
scholarship	kindergarten
extracurricular	public
memorable	enroll

Before most five-year old children enter_____,

their parents decide what school to _____ them

in: a free _____ school open to everyone; a

_____ school that teaches religion in addition to the

standard curriculum; or a _____ school. Parents pay

_____ for children in a private or parochial school.

Well-qualified students may be eligible for a _____

that helps pay for their education.

Children who do not speak English may benefit from a

_____ program in which students are taught in two

languages. In addition to the required subjects, some kids consider

their after-school,_____ activities the most

_____ part of their high school education.

V. Talk about School

Some vocabulary used at school is quite specialized:

Grade Point Average: The "G.P.A." is the complete average of a student's grades received in high school or college. Most schools assign grades on a 4-point scale:

> 4 = A (excellent)
> 3 = B (good)
> 2 = C (satisfactory)
> 1 = D (unsatisfactory)
> 0 = F (no credit)

prerequisite: (*pre-* means "before," and *requi-* relates to "required") a course that students must take before they are eligible to enroll in the next, higher level one

semester: Most colleges divide the year into two equal semesters, each fifteen to eighteen weeks long, between September and June. An optional summer semester of six to eight weeks may also be offered.

units: credit. A full-time college student enrolls in twelve to fifteen units during each of the semesters between September and June. Most courses count for three units; the student attends each class for three hours weekly. Typically about 120 units are required for a B.A. degree.

to drop a class: to quit a course, receiving no grade or credit for it

to add a class: to enroll in a course after regular registration has ended

incomplete: a grade indicating that due to circumstances beyond the student's control, required work in a course was not finished. When the work is done, a grade is given, and the student receives units of credit for the course. If the work is not finished, the incomplete grade changes to an *F* or *No credit*.

to transfer: to change from one school to another. A student must request that units of credit for courses taken will be granted by the new school. Courses are "transferable" if the material covered in them is equivalent at both schools.

VI. Discuss It

Think about the following ideas so that you'll be prepared to talk about them in class.

1. Choose one of the topics listed below and explain how the educational system works in your native country. (More than one student may talk about each topic, as long as different countries are being described. This will prevent repetition. Or, students may organize panel discussions so that several people contribute to the explanation of each topic.)

    A. the primary school system for children

    B. the secondary school system

    C. the college and university system

    D. vocational schools

    E. religious schools

    F. the importance of exams

    G. cheating and its consequences

    H. teacher/student roles and relationships (For example: What names do teachers and students use for each other? What attitudes are they expected to have toward each other? How do they dress?)

    I. _?_ (Your own topic that relates to this unit)

2. Many parents enroll their children in preschool to give them a head start before they begin kindergarten. Other parents say that youngsters should simply play before they start school, enjoying their early years of childhood at home without any academic pressures. What do you think is best?

3. With a partner or in groups, discuss your opinions about whether the following ideas show typical American attitudes toward education. Put *Yes* if you think they do, *No* if you think that they don't. Compare your results with your classmates'.

a. _____ It is more important to study the past than the present and future.

b. _____ Teachers should treat all students equally.

c. _____ It is impolite for a student to ask the teacher a question.

d. _____ Debating various opinions in the classroom can be good.

e. _____ The most important part of education is earning a diploma or degree.

f. _____ Students are expected to learn how to learn.

g. _____ Teachers should never admit that they do not know something, or that they have made a mistake.

h. _____ The best students are young.

i. _____ Students should demonstrate their ability to form original, independent opinions.

4. In many countries, getting an education is a privilege only a few children are allowed. In the United States, kids must attend school until at least age sixteen. Why do you suppose education is required? Do you think that is a good idea, or should parents decide whether or not their children should become educated?

5. The school years are very competitive for earning good grades, for playing sports, for being popular with friends. Do you think this is too much pressure on children and teenagers, or is this good preparation for adult life? Do students in your native country face more or less pressure to succeed than students in the United States do?

6. In some countries, students take one very difficult exam that determines who is eligible for high school or college. In the United States, many factors are considered for college admission, including students' grades, extracurricular activities and test scores. Which system do you think is more fair and effective? Can you suggest a better way for deciding which children should be admitted to college?

7. On an American college campus, young couples may display their affection for each other by holding hands, kissing or hugging. Is similar behavior common in your native country? Do you think such openness is good, or does it seem inappropriate? In the United States, friends may hug each other in a brief greeting, but almost never do people of the same sex link arms or hold hands unless they are gay or lesbian (homosexual). How does that compare to accepted behavior in your native country?

VII. Use It

The best way to learn English is to use it. Doing these activities will give you lots of practice in English.

1. Visit a private, public or parochial school. Get information about the school's special programs, its enrollment requirements and its tuition cost.

2. Contact a school district and request information about their independent home study program. What are the requirements?

3. Interview at least five Americans, asking them to evaluate the ideas listed in discussion topic #7 above. Report the results to the class.

4. Volunteer to tutor school children.

5. At the transfer center or library at your school, find information about your state's college and university system. Research the admission requirements, tuition and financial aid programs.

6. At the transfer center or library at your school, find information about private colleges and universities in your area. If there are several colleges near you, have each student research one. Compare the admission requirements, tuition and financial aid programs.

7. Have each student get information about a service or club at your school. Be prepared to explain what the service or club does, who is eligible, and what it costs. Possibilities include but are not limited to:

A. student health services	J. tutoring
B. student newspaper or yearbook	K. counseling
C. student government	L. financial aid
D. scholarship information	M. computer lab
E. library/media center	N. intercollegiate sports
F. foreign students club	O. transfer center
G. work/study jobs on campus	P. exercise equipment
H. finding off-campus employment	Q. child care
I. political or environmental club	R. writing center/lab

8. Lead the class in singing the *ABC*'s. The words and music are provided in the Appendix.

VIII.   Debate It

Form debate teams that argue *pro* or *con* on the following topics. After listening to the teams' arguments, students in the rest of the class may ask questions of the teams, and then vote *pro* or *con* in secret ballot.

1. School children should wear uniforms.

2. Except for foreign language instruction, English should be the only language used in American classrooms.

3. To make up for past discrimination, colleges should make admission easier for members of disadvantaged groups.

4. Debate a topic you choose that relates to this unit. State the idea in one sentence so that people can argue pro or con.

IX. Consider the Proverbs

Guess what each of these sayings means. Then, give an example that illustrates each one. Be prepared to share it with the class. Does your native language have any of the same proverbs? If so, compare them.

1. Give a man a fish, and he eats for a day. Teach him how to fish, and he eats for the rest of his life.
2. Rome wasn't built in a day.
3. Practice makes perfect.
4. You can lead a horse to water, but you can not make it drink.
5. Well begun is half done.

5

Getting a Job

I. Get Ready

A. Before you watch the video,

- list your personal strengths.

- name at least two jobs that would be ideal for you.

- name at least two things you can do to prepare yourself for those jobs.

- pose a question you have about getting a job in the United States. If your question is not answered in the video, ask your teacher. Your teacher may tell you the answer, or refer you to an information source so you can get the answer yourself and share it with the class.

B. To improve your comprehension of the video, review this vocabulary:

retail - the sales to a consumer
aptitude - an ability
blue-collar - relating to jobs that require physical work
white-collar - relating to office or professional jobs that do not require much physical work
reliable - trustworthy
recruiter - a person who looks for others to work at a company or a branch of the military

temporary - for a short time

permanent - for a long time

security - stability; assurance that a job will continue

classified section - a newspaper's advertisements for jobs, goods and
    services

internet - the communication system between computers

available - open

resource - a place to get information

workshop - a short class

volunteer - to work for free

a foot in the door - an advantage

appropriately - in the correct way

negotiate - to bargain for

II. Watch the Video

Watch and listen to the video. During the interview with Human Resources Coordinator Pat McCrery, notice how important she says it is to present a good resumé and to prepare well for an interview.

After watching the video, read the text below. It matches the narration.

If you want paid employment, consider many factors before you apply for a job. First, what kind of job would you like? Are you looking for part-time work while you are in school? Many immigrants work at ethnic markets, gas stations, taxi cab companies or fast food restaurants while they improve their English. Do you want experience relating to a future career? For example, working as a retail clerk might teach you a lot about running your own store someday.

If you have not chosen a career, ask a school counselor to give you an aptitude test that shows your skills and preferences. Set your professional goals and plan how you will achieve them. If you like to work outside and enjoy using your hands, you might want a blue-collar job such as a gardener, delivery person, mechanic, or heavy equipment operator.   If you prefer to work indoors and use your thinking skills more than your physical abilities, you might be happier in a white-collar job, such as a librarian, accountant or optician.

On average, college graduates earn twice as much as workers who have only a high school diploma. The United States has a knowledge-based economy.

After you have decided what kind of job you want, consider the costs involved for you. Do you have reliable transportation? Will you need to buy new clothes? If you have children, can you make affordable arrangements for child care?

Consider the income you expect to earn on the job. In general, blue collar jobs pay an hourly wage only for the hours you work. Professional white collar jobs usually provide a salary—the same amount weekly or monthly—regardless of the number of hours you work.

In addition to income, compare the benefits different employers offer. Health insurance can mean a huge savings to you and your family. Profit-sharing allows you to gain from the company's success. Another financial consideration is whether or not you will get paid vacation and sick leave. Does the company offer a pension plan to help workers prepare for their retirement? Recruiters will be happy to explain the advantages of choosing a career in the military.

It is increasingly common for employees to be hired on a temporary basis if permanent jobs are not available. Sometimes temporary positions lead to permanent ones, but most of them do not provide benefits or job security.

A good place to start looking for a position is in the newspaper's classified section, called the Want Ads. On the internet you can find information about local as well as distant opportunities. If you're lucky, a friend may tell you about an available position and recommend you for it. Your school may have a placement center that advertises jobs on campus and in the community. Another useful resource is your state's employment office, sometimes called the Employment Development Department. Some offer free workshops on how to get a job. You'll find listings for many available positions, and a job counselor will help you match your skills with current job openings.

Some people volunteer at a place they hope to get a paid job in the future. As volunteers, they learn more about the workplace, and they improve their skills. When a paid position becomes available, they already have a foot in the door.

If you get called for an interview, try to predict what questions you will be asked. Practice answering those questions with a friend role-playing with you. Dress appropriately for the interview, and be sure to arrive on time. Shake hands firmly with the interviewer as you smile and make eye contact.

Most companies want employees with good communication skills since almost all jobs require interacting with other people. At the interview, demonstrate that you listen well and speak clearly. Answer questions fully in a strong voice to show your self-confidence and enthusiasm for the job. Unless the interviewer brings up the topic of wages or salary, avoid asking about it. Once the job is offered to you, then you can negotiate the pay.

Good luck!

III. Understand It

A. Enlarging your vocabulary improves your comprehension. Each unit contains a different activity for learning vocabulary. Try each way at least once. As you study new words, repeat the activities that work best for you.

The instructor assigns a vocabulary word to each student. Then each student composes a question using any form of that word. The question should get more than a yes/no answer. For example, you might ask: "During the last few weeks, what have you _negotiated_ for?" After everyone has composed a question, the students sit in a circle and number off 1, 2, 1, 2, etc. Then, number 1 asks number 2 the question s/he composed, and number 2 asks number 1 the question s/he composed. Answer each other's questions. After about two minutes, the instructor calls "stop." Number 2's stay seated, and the number 1's stand up and move to the left. They sit down, and the process is repeated, with the new partners asking and answering each other's questions. Keep rotating until the number 1's have gone all the way around the circle.

B. With a partner, take turns asking these questions and answering them in complete sentences.

1. What are some places many immigrants find work?
2. What kind of test might help you choose a career?
3. What are at least two examples of blue collar jobs?
4. What are at least two examples of white collar jobs?
5. How much do college graduates earn on average compared to people with only a high school diploma?
6. What are three costs involved in being employed?
7. What type of pay is given to most blue collar workers?
8. What type of pay is given to most white collar workers?
9. What are examples of at least two benefits some employers give?
10. Who looks for new people to join the military?
11. What jobs sometimes lead to permanent positions?
12. What are two disadvantages of temporary jobs?
13. Where does a newspaper list job openings?
14. Where can you find out about opportunities in distant places?
15. What do some school placement centers do?
16. What services are provided by the state employment development department?
17. What are at least two benefits of volunteering?
18. What are two things you can do to prepare for a job interview?
19. What are at least two things you should try to do at the interview?
20. When should you negotiate the pay?

IV. Prepare a Resumé

Follow these directions to prepare a resumé. In addition, practice explaining the information aloud so that you could easily remember it during an interview.

Type your resumé neatly, with no errors, on one sheet of plain paper. Make several copies of it so that you will have one to give to each of the places you apply for a job.

At the top, type your name, address, phone number and e-mail address if you have one. Then, use these headings to organize your information:

Position Desired: Write the name of the job you are applying for.

Experience: If this will be your first paid job, do not even write this heading on your resumé unless you can list volunteer positions. If you have worked before, list your most recent job first. Include for each job:

- the dates of employment
- the name and address of the place where you worked, and the name and phone number of your supervisor
- the name of the job you had
- your main responsibilities

Education: List your most recent education first. Include:

- the dates you attended each school
- the name and address of each school
- your major (the main courses you studied)

Personal Information: If you think it will help you, list any or all of this information. Leave information out if you think it might hurt your chances.

- honors, awards
- clubs, organizations you belong to
- legal status in the United States
- military service
- willingness to relocate (move)
- languages in addition to English that you speak, read and write
- condition of health

References: Usually applicants write "available upon request." If your prospective employer wants to ask other people about you, s/he will request you to give names of people to recommend you. Good choices are past employers and teachers. Be sure to ask them first if they are willing to serve as references for you.

V.   Communicate Well

A. Body Language

You have only one chance to make a first impression. When you meet an employer, how can you communicate in a positive way?

Body language is the information given by your physical behavior. For most Americans, the body language during an introduction that suggests a positive attitude includes:

- eye contact
- a confident smile
- a firm, brief hand shake

When you are seated for an interview,

- lean forward, and do not cross your arms
- show that you are listening actively by nodding your head, saying "mm-hm," and maintaining eye contact

Verbal Language includes what you say and how you say it. Some employers comment about two problems in talking with non-native speakers: 1) their accents may make them difficult to understand; 2) their soft voices make them hard to hear.

When you interview,

- state your first and last name slowly and clearly
- speak in a strong voice
- answer questions in several sentences, not just a few words, to show that you can communicate well in English and that you are enthusiastic about the job

To practice making a good first impression, have students stand up, walk around the room, and introduce themselves to other class members. Use each other's names, and shake hands firmly as you smile and look at each other. Every thirty seconds, a designated person will blow a whistle. Then everyone will find another partner and practice the introductions again.

B. Holding the Floor

When speakers "hold the floor," they show that they have not finished speaking. One way to do this is by saying "um" while they think of what to say next. Also, raising the pitch of the voice shows that the sentence is not yet complete, and the listener should wait for the speaker to finish. At the end of a sentence, a speaker's voice falls.

Listen to your instructor read the following examples, inserting "and" before the last idea listed. Imitate your instructor's intonation.

Then work with a partner to revise the list in each sentence by removing or adding ideas. Raise your voice at the end of the listed words until you get to the last one, where your voice should fall. (Remember that "and" always comes before the last idea in a list.) Take turns with your partner, one of you listing the job duties, and the other answering at the appropriate time, "I believe I can do this job well."

1. The job requires ... (lifting, sorting, weighing).

2. You need experience in ... (keyboarding, filing, answering the phone, greeting customers).

3. Promotions are based on ... (evaluations, length of employment, overall job performance).

4. You are expected to come to work ... (every day, on time, dressed appropriately, feeling ready to work).

5. To succeed as a team, you must ... (cooperate, share ideas, listen to others, be willing to try new things).

VI. Discuss It

Think about the following ideas so that you'll be prepared to talk about them in class.

1. Did you have career goals when you came to the United States? Have you achieved any of them?

2. What are your career goals for next year, for five years from now, for ten years from now?

3. If you could have any job, what would you choose? Why?

4. Some people say that anyone willing to work hard can succeed in America. Other people say that only white men born in the United States really have a good chance. What do you think?

5. If you were interviewing for a job in your native country, in what ways would you act differently than if you were interviewing in the United States?

6. In your native language, is it polite to interrupt someone who is speaking? What should you do if you are interrupted? When speaking English, is it ok to interrupt someone else?

7. Working with a partner, create a list of adjectives that describe a good employee. Then, take turns giving specific examples of your experience at a job or in school when you demonstrated each of those traits. For example, an adjective might be "reliable." You are reliable when you show up for class, complete your homework on time, or can be trusted with a key at your workplace.

VII. Use It

The best way to learn English is to use it. Doing these activities will give you lots of practice in English.

1. Find out if your school offers a service learning program in which students can volunteer to work at a church, school, community agency or workplace. The employer benefits from students' skills, and students benefit by having a chance to practice their English, learn more about the workplace, and gain experience to add to their resumés. If your school does not have a program, you might decide to volunteer at a place you know about so that you can gain valuable experience and help your community at the same time.

2. At the school career center or in the library, find examples of resumés. Select several to bring to the class.

3. Invite several staff members of your school to come to class and answer students' questions about work life.

4. Get information about a job or career that interests you. You might go to your school career center, a library or your state employment office. If you can, interview someone who has a job similar to the one you are interested in. Be prepared to tell the class:

- why this career interests you
- what education or training is needed
- starting wages or salary
- availability of positions
- opportunity for advancement

5. The following questions are typical ones asked at a job interview. In preparation for an interview, answer each question in one to five complete sentences. Practice giving your answers in front of a mirror, recording them on tape, or explaining them to a friend. In class, with your teacher or a classmate playing the role of interviewer, answer the questions. Have other students watch you and give suggestions. Videotape your interview. Notice at least two things that you did well, and two things that need improvement. Remember that "practice makes perfect."

1. What position are you applying for?

_____

_____

2. Why have you chosen to apply for this job?

_____

_____

3. Why are you leaving your present job, or why did you leave your last job?

_____

_____

4. Can you bring any special skills to this job?

_____

_____

5. Do you plan to continue your education?

_____

_____

6. Tell us something about yourself.

_____

_____

7. What do you see yourself doing five years from now?

_____

_____

8. What are your strongest points?

_____

_____

9. What are your weakest points?

_____

_____

10. What would you like to ask us?

_____

_____

VIII. Debate It

Form debate teams that argue *pro* or *con* on the following topics. After listening to the teams' arguments, students in the rest of the class may ask questions of the teams, and then vote *pro* or *con* in secret ballot.

1. Related experience should count just as much as a college degree when someone is applying for a job or promotion.

2. In the United States, success means money.

3. To make up for past discrimination, employers should give preference to applicants from under-represented groups.

4. Debate a topic you choose that relates to this unit. State the idea in one sentence so that people can argue pro or con.

IX. Consider the Proverbs

Guess what each of these sayings means. Then, give an example that illustrates each one. Be prepared to share it with the class. Does your native language have any of the same proverbs? If so, compare them.

1. Don't put all your eggs in one basket.
2. Nothing ventured, nothing gained.
3. Actions speak louder than words.
4. The grass always looks greener on the other side of the fence.
5. Where there's a will, there's a way.

6

Working

I. Get Ready

A. Before you watch the video, work with a partner to -

-   list qualities in an ideal worker.

-   list qualities in an ideal student.

-   state your career goals, being as specific as you can.

-   pose a question you have about working in the United States. If your question is not answered in the video, ask your teacher. Your teacher may tell you the answer, or refer you to an information source so you can get the answer yourself and share it with the class.

B. To improve your comprehension of the video, review this vocabulary:

appropriately - in the right way for the situation
emphasize - to stress
set your sights - to aim
downsize - to make a company smaller
lay off - to dismiss a worker due to an employer's downsizing
moonlight - to work a second job
strike - workers' refusal to work
file - to turn in or send
withhold - to take part of a worker's pay for taxes

gross - full pay, before taxes have been taken out
net - partial pay, after taxes have been taken out
pension - the income given to a retired worker
retirees - people who have chosen not to work any more

II.   Watch the Video

Watch and listen to the video.   During the interview with Information Specialist Wayne Disher, notice how important he says it is to have a positive attitude.

After watching the video, read the text below.   It matches the narration.

When you find a job, you deserve congratulations.   The next challenge is to keep it!

You must come to work every day, on time, dressed appropriately and feeling ready to work.   Many workplaces do not allow smoking.   If you need to smoke during work hours, plan to do it outside on your breaks.

To be a valued employee, keep a positive attitude, and get along with other people.   When you are evaluated, emphasize what you have learned.   If you make a mistake, admit it.   You are responsible for yourself.   Set your sights high, work hard, and you will succeed.

Some companies downsize, reducing the number of employees in order to save money.   If you are laid off or hurt on the job, you will probably be eligible for insurance money through your Employment Development Department.

Increasing numbers of people are working at home on their own computers. If they are self-employed, they may like being their own boss.   Everyone benefits from one less car in commute traffic.

Few people stay in one job for their entire working life.   Many go to school to train for a new career.   As society changes, so does the need for employees in various jobs.   Employment is now growing in service jobs such as sales, security, teaching and social work.   Technically-trained people such as engineers are in great demand.

The medical field includes physicians, nurses, dentists, pharmacists and optometrists.   Veterinarians take care of animals.   The construction industry gives carpenters, roofers and painters the satisfaction of building things with their own hands. People who moonlight work one job during the day, for example as a shipping clerk, karate instructor or film processor, and they hold another job in the evening or on weekends, perhaps as a musician, security guard or food server.

People who like an office environment may enjoy working as a receptionist, secretary, stock broker, teller or manager. People who prefer to be outdoors might work as a mail carrier, tree surgeon, window washer or grounds keeper. Those preferring indoor hands-on work might choose a job as a baker, chef, hairdresser, barber, printer, wood worker or mechanic. Fire fighters and police officers face danger as part of their daily jobs in public safety.

In some jobs, you may join a union. Union leaders bargain with a company's management about wages and working conditions. If labor's demands are not satisfied, the union may call a strike.

All workers must pay tax on their earnings. File your income tax return with the Internal Revenue Service, the I.R.S, by April 15. Many employers withhold part of your gross pay and give it directly to the I.R. S. You take home your net pay. Filling out income tax returns can be confusing, but some libraries offer free assistance.

As you get older, retirement and pension programs may become important for you. Almost all workers contribute to Social Security, the federal insurance program for retirees.

Part of work life is the traditional lunch hour. Many people eat at work with their friends. Some go to a restaurant, and others prefer just to read a book while eating a bag lunch.

A full-time job is usually forty hours a week, but work has to be done for our homes and families, too. We need to shop at grocery stores, prepare meals and wash dishes. Vacuuming and doing laundry are other household chores that must be done. All parents, whether or not they work outside the home, must find time to give love and attention to their children.

III. Understand It

A. Enlarging your vocabulary improves your comprehension. Each

unit contains a different activity for learning vocabulary. Try each way at least once. As you study new words, repeat the activities that work best for you.

Write each vocabulary word on a slip of paper, and put the papers in a basket. Form teams of three people, and have one person from each team randomly choose a slip of paper and look at the word on it, without showing it to anyone else. Then, each person who chose a slip will draw a picture that represents the word. Using the picture as their only clue, the team tries to guess the word. After they succeed, another team member selects a new word from the basket. Continue until the basket is empty. To lengthen the game, add the names of various jobs.

B. With a partner, take turns asking these questions and answering them in complete sentences.

1. What are four basic things you must do to keep your job?
2. What should you emphasize during an evaluation?
3. If you are laid off or hurt on the job, where can you get insurance money?
4. In what area is employment growing?
5. What are two examples of technically-trained people?
6. What are five examples of jobs in the medical field?
7. What are three examples of jobs in the construction industry?
8. What does it mean to moonlight?
9. What are five examples of office jobs?
10. What are three examples of outdoor jobs?
11. What are three examples of indoor, hands-on jobs?
12. What are two examples of dangerous public service jobs?
13. What does a union do?
14. Why would a union call a strike?
15. By what date must workers file an income tax return?
16. What is the name for your full pay?
17. What is the name for the money you actually take home?
18 What is the federal insurance program for retirees?
19. How many hours a week is a full-time job?
20. What are at least three examples of household chores?

IV. Develop a Positive Attitude

A. Most employers consider a positive attitude the quality they value most in an employee.

In groups, make a list of at least five behaviors or traits that show a person's positive attitude, and a list of traits that show a negative attitude. Compare your group's lists with those made by others. Write all the ideas on the board. Identify at least two positive and negative qualities that you have.

In groups, discuss the following:

1. Have you ever worked with a person who had a negative attitude? What was it like? How were you affected by that person's attitude?

2. Have you ever worked with a person who had a positive attitude? What was it like? How were you affected by that person's attitude?

3. What can a person do to develop positive behaviors? List specific suggestions. Share your group's ideas with the class.

B. Learn how to disagree. Successful employees usually express complaints and deal with disagreements clearly yet courteously. Here are some tips on how you can, too:

- **Use "I" statements instead of "You" statements.**

Here are three examples:

- Instead of "<u>You</u> don't pay attention to my ideas,"
  say "<u>I</u> feel that my ideas deserve more attention."

- Instead of "<u>You</u> don't tell me what you expect me to do,"
  say, "<u>I</u> need a clearer explanation of what <u>I</u> am expected to do."

- Instead of "<u>You</u> are wrong,"
  say "<u>I</u> see it differently" or "<u>I</u> have had a different experience."

Replace these "you" statements with "I" statements:

1) You take my ideas without giving me credit for them.

_____

2) You have a stupid idea.

_____

3) You blame me for mistakes that other people make.

_____

* **Avoid "always" and "never" statements.**

Here are three examples:
* Instead of "You <u>never</u> notice when I do something right; you <u>always</u> criticize me when I do something wrong,"
    say "I deserve recognition when I do things right, not just criticism when I make a mistake."

* Instead of "You <u>never</u> pay attention to what I want,"
    say "I want to be included in decision making."

* Instead of "You <u>always</u> give me more than my share of the work,"
    say "I think that I am doing more than my fair share."

Use "I" and delete "always" or "never" as you rephrase these complaints:

1) You never remember to include my vacation time in the schedule.

_____

2) You always expect the impossible!

_____

3) You always come in late and expect me to cover for you, but you never do the same for me.

_____

V. Discuss It

Think about the following ideas so that you'll be prepared to talk about them in class.

1.   Some men say it's hard for them to work for a female boss. Is it hard for women to work for a male boss? What does "stereotype" mean? How does "stereotype" apply to male/female relations on the job?

2. If a union calls a strike, often the company tries to hire "scabs" (non-union workers) to fill the jobs until the strike is over. Would you work as a scab, or would you support union workers on strike?

3. Compare the importance of various jobs in America with the status they have in your native country. Some examples might be lawyers, teachers, athletes, musicians or priests.

4. Many truck drivers are paid more than nurses, and football stars earn more than the President of the United States. Why do you think this is so, and is it fair?

5. Experience the job of manager. With a partner, role-play telling an employee that the company is downsizing and his/her job is being eliminated. Be courteous and understanding. Give the laid-off worker specific suggestions to help deal with unemployment.

6. Three out of four American adults of working age have paid employment. It is common for both a husband and wife to work full time. Who should be responsible for household chores and child care?

7. Do you think the saying is true that "Money can't buy happiness"? Why or why not?

8. In your native country, do most people stay employed by the same company for their whole careers? Do you think workers benefit from job changes? Do their employers? Why or why not?

9. List as many reasons as you can why a person might lose a job. Which reasons can an employee control?

10. In many companies, employees are expected to cooperate as members of a team assigned to complete a task. List the qualities of a good team member.

VI. Use It

The best way to learn English is to use it. Doing these activities will give you lots of practice in English.

1. Ask a worker you know if you may accompany him or her to the workplace for a couple of hours. Make a list of questions you want to answer based on your observation. Take notes on what you observe, and share your information with the class.

2. In class, create a short list of questions that you would like to have working people answer for you. Then, interview at least three workers. Explain your findings to the class.

3. Make a tape. Record your own informal tips on how to keep a job as if you were explaining it to someone recently hired in the United States. You may use notes, but do not read something you have written word for word. Your instructor may listen to your tape, or ask you to exchange tapes with a classmate. At the end of your classmate's tape, record at least three positive comments about the explanation.

4. Working in teams, study an aspect of work life. To get your information, you may need to do research in the library, at your school's career center, or at public agencies. Teach the class what you have learned. Choose from these topics:

    a.   how to complete income tax forms
    b.   Social Security for retirees
    c.   unemployment insurance: who is eligible, how to get it, and how much it is worth

d. disability insurance: who is eligible, how to get it, and how much it is worth

e. workers' compensation: who is eligible, how to get it, and how much it is worth

f. Occupational Safety and Health Administration: what it does

g. sexual harassment: what it is, and how to avoid it

h. pro's and con's of joining a union

i. the cost of health insurance

j. average salaries for ten jobs in your area

k. employment trends for the next two years in your area

l. seniority: what it is, and how it affects employees

m. your own topic that relates to life on the job

5. With a partner or in groups, discuss your opinions about whether the following ideas show typical American attitudes toward the workplace. Put *Yes* if they generally do, *No* if they generally don't, and *Sometimes* if you feel that the situation determines what is appropriate. Compare your results with the rest of the class.

Then, have each student ask at least three employed Americans outside of the class to evaluate the ideas. Report the results.

a. _____ To show how smart they are, employees should avoid asking questions.

b. _____ Managers should treat all workers the same.

c. _____ Workers should give their opinion only if the supervisor asks them for it.

d. _____ Open disagreement at the workplace can be good.

e. _____ Neither the boss nor an employee should ever have to admit they made a mistake.

f. _____ Workers are expected to learn new things all the time.

g. _____ The most important part of a job is earning money.

h. _____ Employees should have equal opportunity for promotion.

i. _____ Every job should be a step up in career advancement.

j. _____ The best employees always support the opinions of their supervisor.

VII. Debate It

Form debate teams that argue *pro* or *con* on the following topics. After listening to the teams' arguments, students in the rest of the class may ask questions of the teams, and then vote *pro* or *con* in secret ballot.

1. Both a husband and wife can have paid employment outside the home and be good parents, too.

2. Employers should be allowed to give workers drug tests any time they are on the job.

3. Seniority privileges provide well-deserved protection to long-term workers.

4. Debate a topic you choose that relates to this unit. State the idea in one sentence so that people can argue pro or con.

VIII. Consider the Proverbs

Guess what each of these sayings means. Then, give an example that illustrates each one. Be prepared to share it with the class. Does your native language have any of the same proverbs? If so, compare them.

1. Many hands make light work.
2. Slow and steady wins the race.
3. Haste makes waste.
4. A penny saved is a penny earned.
5. A bird in hand is worth two in the bush.

7

Leisure

I. Get Ready

A. Before you watch the video, work with a partner to -

- name at least ten sports popular in the United States.

- name at least two American athletes.

- name at least five weekend activities that people do for fun.

- pose a question you have about leisure in the United States. If your question is not answered in the video, ask your teacher. Your teacher may tell you the answer, or refer you to an information source so you can get the answer yourself and share it with the class.

B. To improve your comprehension of the video, review this vocabulary:

nap - a short sleep during the day
hammock - a hanging bed with cords attached to supports at each end
polish - to rub a surface to make it shiny
bumper sticker - a strip of paper attached to a car
accomplishments - achievements
custom - original, unique
"fill 'em up" - to put gasoline in cars
brunch - a combination of breakfast and lunch, especially on Sunday
bite to eat - a snack
obesity - extreme overweight

flea market - open-air market where people bargain for prices

mall - large, covered shopping center

do-it-yourselfer - an amateur who makes or repairs things instead of hiring a professional

maintain - to keep in good condition

identify - to name

rink - a smooth, large, ice-covered area, often inside an arena

spoil - to ruin

II. Watch the Video

Watch and listen to the video. During the interview with jogger Amanda Morgan, notice that she says exercise keeps her energy level up.

After watching the video, read the text below. It matches the narration.

There are as many ways to spend leisure time as there are people to enjoy it. For some people, the best way to spend an afternoon is to sit, relax and read a book. Some prefer a nap in a hammock, or a casual get-together with friends and family.

Cars are important in the lives of most Americans. They buy cars, sell them, wash and polish them. When the car breaks down, they may work on it themselves, or call for help. Sometimes a tow truck must take it to a mechanic.

Bumper stickers on some cars show their owners' opinions, their favorite team, the college they attended, or their kids' accomplishments. Some drivers pay extra for a personalized license plate, get a custom paint job, or fix up an old car. Motorists "fill 'em up," buckle their seat belts, and travel the country's four million miles of roads. Only a small minority prefer riding a motorcycle to driving a car.

Just about everybody loves to eat, whether it's a dinner at home, lunch at a fast food restaurant, pizza with friends, or a Sunday brunch. There's always time for a quick bite to eat. In fact, American eating habits have caused obesity to become a major health problem.

To improve their health, some people take exercise classes offered at schools on the weekends. Others join health and fitness clubs to stay in shape. Some people exercise by bicycling, jogging, golfing, roller blading, playing tennis, doing karate, fencing, horseback riding, or simply walking the dog. Many people have fun taking short hikes while they identify different kinds of birds.

Shopping is a common leisure activity. Yard sales and flea markets attract bargain hunters. Indoor malls make shopping comfortable any time of year.

Many homeowners are do-it-yourselfers. Instead of hiring someone to do the job, they buy supplies and do it on their own. Gardening and yard work are a routine part of maintaining a home.

Sports are very popular, such as basketball, baseball, bowling, bicycle racing and volleyball. Many people love the water. They may go to the beach, or they might go boating, row on a crew team, ride a jet ski, go canoeing, kayaking, fishing, windsurfing, water-skiing, sailing, surfing or swimming.

Most Americans watch three or four hours of TV every day. For an evening's entertainment, they may rent a video, go to the movies or a concert. Friends may get together for a drink at a bar, listen to a band, go to a party or go dancing.

In a few states, gambling is legal. If you're twenty-one or older, you might want to give your luck a try.

For many Americans, a vacation offers a chance to travel, eat in restaurants and relax in hotels. For others, music festivals provide a weekend's escape from the routines of daily life. Lovers of the outdoors may choose to go camping in their leisure time, sleeping under the stars or putting up a tent. A campfire keeps them warm as they enjoy being close to nature.

In winter, skiers head for the slopes for cross-country or downhill skiing. Indoor rinks make ice skating possible all year long.

No matter what leisure activities you try, just don't spoil your fun by charging more than you can afford!

III. Understand It

A. Enlarging your vocabulary improves your comprehension. Each

unit contains a different activity for learning vocabulary. Try each way at least once. As you study new words, repeat the activities that work best for you.

Have every student bring at least two pictures or objects to class, each relating to one leisure activity described in this unit. Tape the pictures to the board and place the objects on a table. Put numbers by each one.

Set a timer and allow students to write the names and numbers of each activity or object. Then have an oral contest. A student or teacher can call out a number, and students compete to be the first to name the leisure activity that matches the number.

B. With a partner, take turns asking these questions and answering them in complete sentences.

1.   What makes a good place to take a nap?
2.   If a car breaks down, how can you get it to a mechanic?
3.   What do bumper stickers show?
4.   How many miles of paved roads does the United States have?
5.   What are some typical meals?
6.   What has become a major health problem in America?
7.   How do some people improve their health?
8.   What clubs might they join?
9.   What are at least five ways some people exercise?
10. Where do many shoppers find bargains?
11. Who are typical do-it-yourselfers?
12. What activities are part of maintaining a home?
13. What are some popular sports?
14. What are at least five popular water sports?
15. How much TV do most Americans watch?
16. What is an example of a typical evening's entertainment?
17. How old do you have to be to gamble?
18. What activity appeals to people who love the outdoors?
19. What are two types of skiing?
20. Where can people ice skate all year long?

IV. Solve It

Many people enjoy working on crossword puzzles in their leisure time. Work with a partner to solve this one.

Across

5 physical activity
6 a hanging bed
11 to name
12 time off, relaxation
13 indoor shopping center

Down

1 extreme overweight
2 an outdoor market
3 physical well-being
4 an ice-covered area
7 original
8 part of a car
9 a movie
10 breakfast/lunch

V. Build It Up

To improve your fluency, practice building a sentence by pronouncing it from the final word group.

To get started, identify word groups or phrases in the sentence you are going to practice. Then, try this pattern:

to enjoy it.
as there are people to enjoy it.
to spend leisure time as there are people to enjoy it.
as many ways to spend leisure time as there are people to enjoy it.
There are as many ways to spend leisure time as there are people to enjoy it.

read a book.
relax and read a book.
sit, relax and read a book.
to spend an afternoon is to sit, relax and read a book.
the best way to spend an afternoon is to sit, relax and read a book.
For some people, the best way to spend an afternoon is to sit, relax and
    read a book.

with friends.
get-together with friends.
or a casual get-together with friends.
a nap in a hammock, or a casual get-together with friends.
Some prefer a nap in a hammock, or a casual get-together with friends.

of most Americans.
in the lives of most Americans.
Cars are important in the lives of most Americans.

Follow the pattern, using any sentences from the narration.

VI. Discuss It

Think about the following ideas so that you'll be prepared to talk about them in class.

1. Describe to the class a game or sport that is not played in the United States, but that is popular in your native country.

2. Although watching TV is a common pastime in America, people often complain that many TV shows are stupid and a waste of time. Other people say there are worthwhile educational programs on TV if viewers are willing to look for them. What do you think?

3. In America, recreation and leisure often include drinking alcohol. Alcoholism, illness and drunk driving are common problems. How can alcohol abuse be reduced? Is it a problem in your native country?

4. Compare any example of a leisure activity in your native country with that activity in the United States.

5. Some people say that "Laughter is the best medicine." In groups, consider what the saying means, and whether or not you agree.

6. Students should count off, starting with number one. After reaching the number six, start with one again. Continue the counting until everyone has a number between one and six.

Congratulations, everyone is a winner! Imagine that your number indicates which of the prizes you have won, listed below. Get into groups of students with the same number, and discuss the plans you each have for your prizes.

1) You have won the new car of your choice, free! What kind would you choose, and why?

2) You have won a free two-week vacation! Where would you like to go, and what would you do?

3) You have won a year's free lessons to learn the game or sport of your choice! What will it be? Why?

4) You have won free tickets to the concert or sporting event of your choice! What would you like to see?

5) You have won a free shopping trip to the store of your choice! For two hours, you can select whatever you want. Where will you shop, and what will you choose?

6) You have won the home of your choice! Where will your house be, and what will it be like?

VII. Use It

The best way to learn English is to use it. Doing these activities will give you lots of practice in English. Describe your experiences to

the class, and be prepared to answer their questions.

1.   Try a sport that is new for you. Explain to the class how the sport is played.

2.   Visit a famous landmark near your city, such as a historic site, a mountain, a lake or a river, and explain to the class what you experienced.

3.   Find out about any famous American resort or recreation spot (for example, Disney World, Lake Tahoe, Niagara Falls, any of the National Parks, etc.). Tell the class about the resort's (1) location, (2) special attractions, and (3) activities for visitors.

4.   If you have never been to one, attend a game of professional basketball, baseball, football, golf or tennis, etc.

5.   If you don't know how to swim, sign up for swimming lessons. They will probably be offered at your school, the Parks and Recreation Department, or the YWCA or YMCA.

6.   Attend a concert, go to a dance or visit an art exhibit.

7.   Research a national, state or county park. Then, playing the role of park ranger, encourage the class to visit the park by describing its geographic features and the activities for visitors.

8.   Research the history of automobiles in the United States.

9.   Research the history of the martial arts in the United States. Contact a studio to see if any volunteers will come demonstrate karate to your class.

10. Contact the Department of Motor Vehicles to find out if personalized license plates are available in your state, what they cost, and how they can be ordered.

11. Visit a health and fitness club. Find out about its facilities and its membership dues.

12. Using a guidebook, identify at least fifteen different birds in your

area. Notice their appearance and behavior.

13. Ask your teacher to recommend several current videos or documentaries available at video rental stores or the library. Watch the video and prepare a three-minute summary of it for your classmates.

VIII.   Debate It

Form debate teams that argue *pro* or *con* on the following topics. After listening to the teams' arguments, students in the rest of the class may ask questions of the teams, and then vote *pro* or *con* in secret ballot.

1.   Laws requiring the use of automobile seat belts should be more strongly enforced.

2.   People should become eligible for a driver's license when they reach eighteen years of age.

3.   The government should double the price of gasoline and use the money to fight air pollution.

4.   Debate a topic you choose that relates to this unit. State the idea in one sentence so that people can argue pro or con.

IX.   Consider the Proverbs

Guess what each of these sayings means. Then, give an example that illustrates each one. Be prepared to share it with the class. Does your native language have any of the same proverbs? If so, compare them.

1.   All work and no play makes Jack a dull boy.
2.   Eat, drink and be merry, for tomorrow may never come.
3.   While the cat's away, the mice will play.
4.   You can't have your cake and eat it, too.
5.   An ounce of prevention is worth a pound of cure.

78

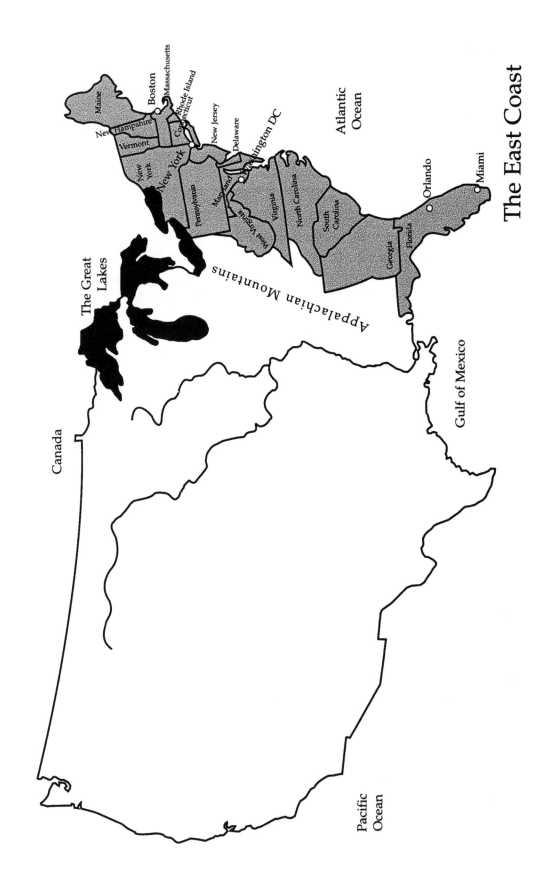

The East Coast

8
The East Coast
Past & Present

I. Get Ready

A. Before you watch the video, work with a partner to -

-   identify five major cities in the East and the states they're located in.

-   identify at least three of the East's geographic features, such as mountains, rivers or lakes.

-   name any famous historical event that took place in the eastern United States.

-   pose a question you have about the geography or history of the eastern United States. If your question is not answered in the video, ask your teacher. Your teacher may tell you the answer, or refer you to the library so you can get the information yourself and share it with the class.

B. To improve your comprehension of the video, review this vocabulary:

subdue - to put down, control

proclaim - to announce

region - an area

foliage - leaves on trees

picturesque - pretty, especially relating to a building or scene

fabric - cloth such as cotton, linen or wool

interior - inside, center

lock - on a canal, an enclosed, gated chamber in which boats can be raised or lowered from one water level to another

Yankee -- in general, an American; sometimes, a northerner

ingenuity - creativity, originality

preserve - to keep

spectacular - beautiful, grand

network - a group of people who communicate with each other

abolitionist - a person who wants to end slavery

metropolitan - urban

symbolize - to represent

glamour - excitement

wildlife - animals living in nature

character - image, identity

II. Watch the Video

Watch and listen to the video. During the interview with historian Debra Barth, notice her explanation of the interaction between Europeans and American Indians, and the general importance of the East Coast in shaping the image of the United States.

After watching the video, read the text below. It matches the narration.

America has long been a land of immigrants. In the seventeenth century, English Puritans crossed the Atlantic to find religious freedom in New England. Many British citizens came to the Colonies because they believed that with bravery and hard work, they could build better lives than they could have had in England.

Conflicts developed between the colonists and England. In 1775, Paul Revere warned Massachusetts residents that armed British troops were coming to subdue them. Thomas Jefferson wrote the Declaration

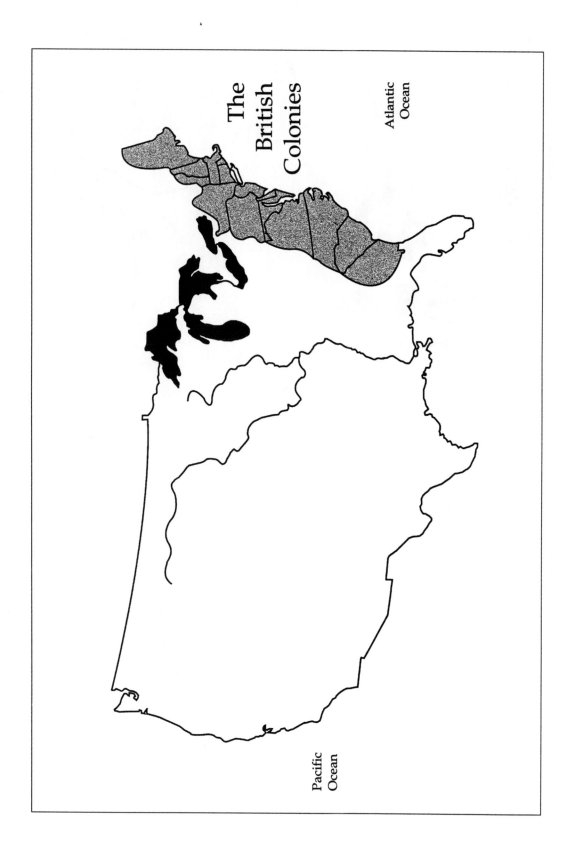

The British Colonies

Atlantic Ocean

Pacific Ocean

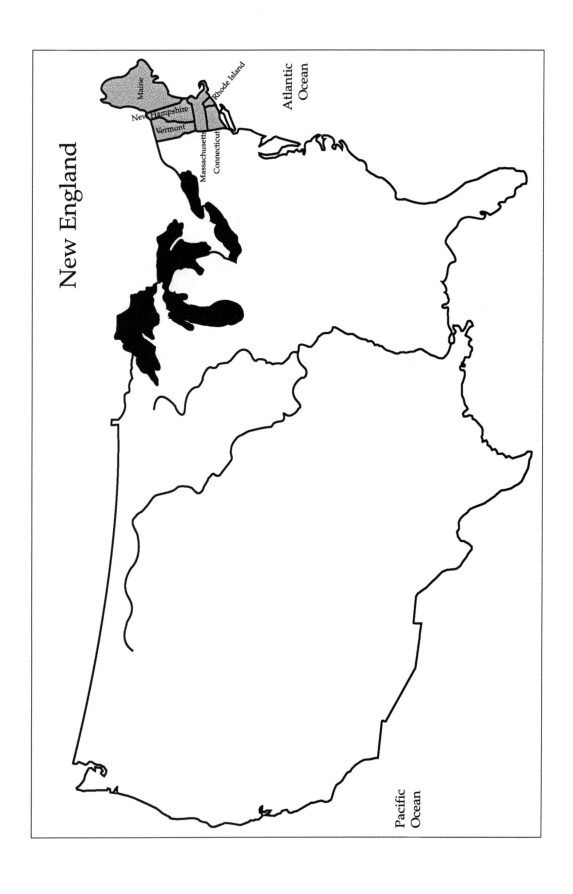

New England

Maine

New Hampshire

Vermont

Massachusetts

Rhode Island

Connecticut

Atlantic Ocean

Pacific Ocean

of Independence, signed on July 4, 1776. It proclaimed that "all men are created equal," each with the right to "life, liberty and the pursuit of happiness." George Washington led the Revolutionary Army to victory against the British, and he became the first President of the United States. Today you can visit Washington's home in Mt. Vernon, and Jefferson's home, Monticello, both in Virginia.

The northeastern United States is still called "New England." The region is known for its beautiful autumn foliage, its picturesque towns, rolling hills, and its long, snowy winters. Fishing, historic whaling and the manufacturing of fabric are the area's best-known industries. Boston, Massachusetts, the largest city in New England, is a center of trade, technology, education and culture.

Completed in 1825, the Erie Canal connected the cities of the East Coast with the Great Lakes and the country's undeveloped interior. The modern Erie Canal follows the same route used by thousands of westward settlers almost two hundred years ago. By a system of locks, the canal climbs over five hundred feet. Its engineers showed "Yankee ingenuity" by creating new technology in order to build the canal through the wilderness.

The canal system passes through Seneca Falls, New York, the birthplace of Women's Rights. A museum preserves the walls of the building in which Elizabeth Cady Stanton demanded equal rights for women, including the right to vote, in 1848. She and Susan B. Anthony dedicated their lives to women's rights. In Seneca Falls, the National Women's Hall of Fame honors women of the past and present.

The Erie Canal ends on Lake Erie, not far from spectacular Niagara Falls, on the New York-Canadian border. Near the canal are many former stations of the underground railroad, a network of northern abolitionists who opened their homes to hide slaves as they were escaping from the southern United States to Canada. The eastern end of the Canal meets the Hudson River which flows to New York City and the Atlantic Ocean. When the Canal was built, New York City began growing into one of the world's major metropolitan centers.

Today New York City has world-famous art museums, theaters and sporting events. The Statue of Liberty, a gift from France in 1886, symbolizes America's traditional welcome to immigrants. Between 1895 and 1924, the reception station at New York's Ellis Island processed twelve million immigrants to the United States.

About two hundred miles south of New York City lies Washington D.C., the nation's capital. There, tourists ride the metro to visit the city's many landmarks, including the White House, the Capitol, the Smithsonian Museum, the Franklin Delano Roosevelt Memorial, and the Vietnam War Memorial. The Lincoln Memorial honors Abraham Lincoln, President during the American Civil War from 1861-1865. The Union Army of the North defeated the Confederate Army of the South, and American slavery ended forever. Arlington National Cemetery near Washington, D.C., was created at the end of the Civil War. The bald eagle symbolizes the strength of the nation.

Today, the warm climate of the South attracts both retirees and vacationers. They may come to enjoy the glamour of Miami Beach or the wildlife of the Everglades where alligators and birds outnumber people. Every year, millions of tourists visit Orlando, Florida to have fun at Disney World and to learn about advances in technology at the Kennedy Space Center.

Rich in both tradition and progress, the East Coast has shaped much of the American character.

III.   Understand It

A.   Enlarging your vocabulary improves your comprehension.   Each unit contains a different activity for learning vocabulary.   Try each way at least once.   As you study new words, repeat the activities that work best for you.

A good way to learn new vocabulary is by sorting words into groups. For example, can you see what each of these groups of words has in common?

group one	*group two*	*group three*
Washington	slow	read
Lincoln	sleep	write
Roosevelt	slam	study
	slur	calculate

Sort the words from this unit's vocabulary list into groups. Compare your groups with those made by your classmates.

B. From the list below, choose the word that means the *opposite*:

subdue   proclaim
interior   picturesque
metropolitan   glamour
network   retirees
ingenuity   preserve

1. _____ whisper
2. _____ ugly
3. _____ exterior
4. _____ rural
5. _____ liberate
6. _____ stupidity
7. _____ workers
8. _____ simplicity
9. _____ lack of communication
10. _____ destroy

C. With a partner, take turns asking these questions and answering them in complete sentences.

1. Why did English Puritans immigrate to America?
2. What did Paul Revere do?
3. Who wrote the Declaration of Independence?
4. When did the United States declare its independence?
5. Who was the first President of the United States?
6. Where was Washington's home?
7. What is the nickname for the northeastern United States?
8. What are some of the area's best-known industries?
9. What did the Erie Canal connect?
10. How does the Canal climb uphill?

11. What city is the birthplace of women's rights?
12. Who were two famous women who fought for women's rights in the nineteenth century?
13. Who used the underground railroad?
14. What does the Statue of Liberty symbolize?
15. Where was a famous immigrant reception station on the East Coast?
16. What is the capital of the United States?
17. What are three landmarks in Washington, D.C.?
18. Who was President during the American Civil War?
19. What symbolizes the United States?
20. What city attracts millions of tourists every year?

IV. Find It

A. Working with a partner, answer the following questions.
1. Which ocean borders the East Coast?
2. What country is to the north of the United States?
3. What gulf borders part of the southern United States?
4. What is the largest mountain range in the eastern United States?
5. What lakes separate part of the northeastern United States from Canada?

B. Practice giving directions.

On the board, draw a large circle to represent a compass showing *north, northeast, east, southeast, south, southwest, west* a n d *northwest.* Then take turns having each student name a city or landmark in the eastern United States. The rest of the class will then name and point in the direction they would need to go to reach that spot from Washington, D.C.

V. Discuss It

Think about the following ideas so that you'll be prepared to talk about them in class.

1. Describe your native city or any other city you know well. Include this information about it:

- population
- educational opportunities
- main industries

- climate
- the pace of life there
- what you like best about it

2. The original American democratic government was considered a radical experiment. Could people govern themselves? Role play an exchange between supporters of the new American form of government and traditionalists who doubt that the general population is capable of democracy.

3. Some Americans believe that space exploration should be a top priority, but others disagree. How important do you think space exploration is? Do citizens benefit from it? Can you think of any consumer products that were originally developed by scientists working on satellites, shuttles, rockets, etc.?

4. Compared to many cultures, American society allows individuals a tremendous amount of freedom. Do you think freedom is always good? Are problems such as crime, drug abuse and a weakening of the family caused by Americans' emphasis on freedom?

5. Some immigrants came to America in order to worship as they wished. Do you think the variety in religions in the United States today enriches the culture, or do you think the variety reduces national unity?

VI. Use It

The best way to learn English is to use it. Doing these activities will give you lots of practice in English.

When you finish your research, share your findings with the class.

1. Contact AMTRAK and get the train schedule and cost for a trip you imagine that would take you to at least four of the places mentioned in this unit.

2. Contact an airline or travel agent and get the airline schedule and cost for a trip you imagine that would take you to at least four of the places mentioned in this unit.

3. Contact a car rental agency and find out the cost for a driving trip that includes at least four of the places mentioned in this unit.

4. Contact a bus line and find out the cost for a trip you imagine that would take you to at least four of the places mentioned in this unit.

5. Choose a place mentioned in this unit that you would like to visit. Research it. In addition to going to the library and talking with people who have been there, you might look for a website on the internet with information about the place you are interested in. Then play the role of travel agent trying to persuade the class to visit, too.

6. Select a historical event mentioned in this unit. After researching it, play the role of a key person, such as Washington, Lincoln or Jefferson. In character, explain what "you" did and why. You may work independently or in groups.

7. Research one of the following topics related to the East so that you can tell the class about it in a brief presentation.

   A.   American Indians in eighteenth century New England
   B.   Mohawk Indians today
   C.   Paul Revere
   D.   the American Revolution
   E.   Thomas Jefferson
   F.   the Declaration of Independence
   G.   George Washington
   H.   the Erie Canal
   I.   the first Women's Rights Convention
   J.   the abolition movement
   K.   the Civil War
   L.   the underground railroad
   M.   Abraham Lincoln
   N.   the National Women's Hall of Fame

O.   Disney World
P.   the Everglades
Q.   alligators
R.   hurricanes
S.   Miami Beach
T.   the Kennedy Space Center

8.   Many Americans have ancestors who passed through Ellis Island. Interview at least five Americans about their ancestry. How many generations before them do they know about? Did any of them enter the United States via Ellis Island?

9.   Research the life of Elizabeth Cady Stanton, Susan B. Anthony, or any other nineteenth century women's suffrage supporter.

10.   A feminist believes in the equality of men and women. Research the life and beliefs of a contemporary feminist leader such as Gloria Steinem or Betty Friedan.

11. In the nineteenth century, abolitionists demanded an end to slavery. Research the life of an abolitionist such as Frederick Douglass or Harriet Tubman.

12. Research any state in the eastern United States. What was it called before statehood? When did it become a state? What is its capital? What are its best known industries? Does it have any famous universities, museums, National Parks or other points of interest? If possible, interview people who live or lived there.

13. Imagine that a friend from your native country is about to arrive in New York City. During the flight, your friend will listen to a "talking letter" that you have made. For your friend, record on tape your suggestions about interesting places to see and things to do on the East Coast.

14. Most states have nicknames and slogans. For example, New York is called the "Empire State." Research the nicknames of at least ten states in the East and explain their meaning or significance.

15. Ask your instructor to recommend a video relating to the people and events discussed in this unit. For example, your library may have a copy of the Public Broadcasting System's documentary *The Civil War* by Ken Burns. After viewing one of the segments, prepare a brief summary for your classmates. Or, you might watch *Gone with the Wind*, a video of Maureen O'Hara's classic novel set in the South during the Civil War.

16. In the library, get copies of the *Declaration of Independence*, the *Declaration of Women's Rights and Sentiments*, Lincoln's *Gettysburg Address* and the *Preamble* to the Constitution. Select the one that interests you the most. Depending on the number of people in your class, your instructor may ask groups of students to read and discuss different parts of the selected documents. Choose a spokesperson from each group to explain to the class what the group has discussed.

Also, your instructor may dictate all or part of the documents for you to practice writing.

17. People who live in different regions often have unique accents. Research the characteristics of the New England, New York and southern accents. If possible, invite speakers to come to class who can demonstrate the accents, or bring recorded examples.

18. Find out about the population in the East. Research the history of ethnic groups in any major city.

19. Congratulations! A large company has offered you an excellent job at any of their five locations. To select the location you would like best, compare the various cities' cost of living, population, climate, educational and recreational opportunities. Explain to the class why you would choose to live and work in Miami, Atlanta, Washington, D.C., New York City or Boston.

VII.   Debate It

Form debate teams that argue *pro* or *con* on the following topics. After listening to the teams' arguments, students in the rest of the class

may ask questions of the teams, and then vote *pro* **or** *con* **in secret ballot.**

1. As a land of immigrants, the United States will endure as one nation only if newcomers give up their various ethnic traditions and replace them with the language and culture of America.

2. The United States should be open to all immigrants who want to come.

3. Women in the United States now have rights equal with men.

4. Debate a topic you choose that relates to this unit. State the idea in one sentence so that people can argue pro or con.

VIII. Consider the Quotes

Explain what each of these sayings means. Research the historical significance of each speaker and quote.

1. "Give me liberty or give me death!"
    Patrick Henry, Revolutionary War hero

2. "God never made a man good enough to govern other men without their consent."
    Abraham Lincoln, sixteenth President of the United States

3. "Men: their rights and nothing more. Women: their rights and nothing less."
    Susan B. Anthony, leader of the women's suffrage movement

4. "Speak softly, but carry a big stick."
    Theodore Roosevelt, twenty-sixth President of the United States

5. "Don't ask what your country can do for you. Ask what you can do for your country."
    John F. Kennedy, thirty-fifth President of the United States

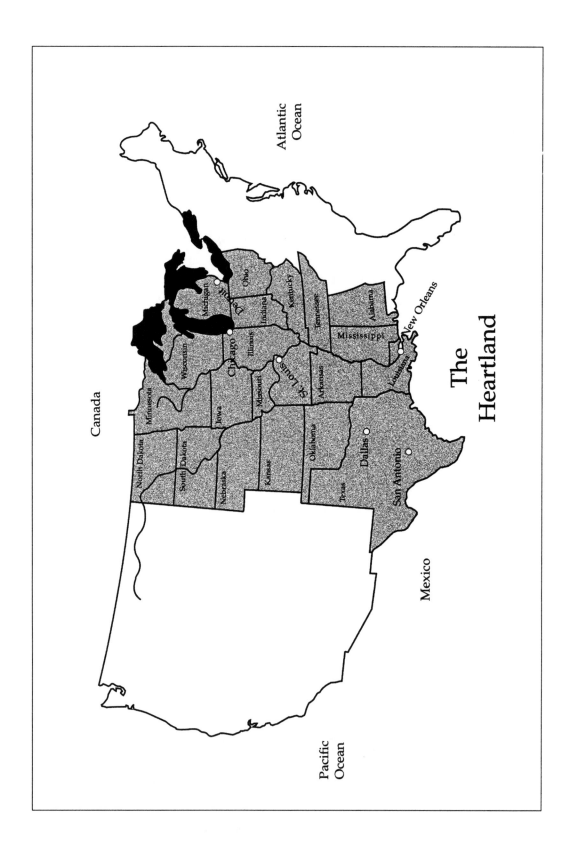

9

The Heartland
Past & Present

I. Get Ready

A. Before you watch the video, work with a partner to -

- identify five major cities in the central United States and the states they're located in.

- list the states bordering the Mississippi River.

- name any famous historical event that especially affected the central United States.

- pose a question you have about the geography or history of the central United States. If your question is not answered in the video, ask your teacher. Your teacher may tell you the answer, or refer you to the library so you can get the information yourself and share it with the class.

B. To improve your comprehension of the video, review this vocabulary:

agricultural - related to farming
patriotic - showing loyalty to one's country

tame - to control (something) so that it is no longer wild

flood - the overflowing of water, covering land that is usually dry

double - to make twice as big

tributary - a river or stream that flows into a larger river or stream

expedition - a lengthy journey made for a particular purpose

acquired - gained

frontier - an undeveloped region with little settlement

adapt - to change

commemorate - to honor or remember something or someone

prairie - extensive, generally level land originally covered with coarse
    grass

Great Plains - the flat land between the Mississippi River and the Rocky
    Mountains

checkerboard - a game board consisting of squares of alternating colors

fertile - productive, creative

barge - a large, flat-bottomed cargo vessel

Dixieland - relating to the southern states

elegant - luxurious

transcontinental - across the continent

cherish - to appreciate very much

II. Watch the Video

Watch and listen to the video. During the interview with Mississippi River Boat Captain Bob Schleiker, notice how important he says it is to respect the power of nature.

After watching the video, read the text below. It matches the narration.

A vast and varied region, the central United States stretches from the Appalachian Mountains in the East to the Rockies in the West. The northern section, often called the Midwest, is primarily agricultural. Midwesterners are known for their small-town friendliness and their love of traditions that may range from such activities as patriotic 4th of July celebrations to old-fashioned pie-eating contests.

Two of the most important midwestern cities are located on the shores of the Great Lakes. Chicago, Illinois is a large center of commerce and transportation. Detroit, Michigan is nicknamed the "Motor City" because it's the home of America's automobile industry. Like states anywhere in the country, midwestern states each have their own identity. For example, Wisconsin is best known for its dairy products, especially cheese. And if you're looking for sweet corn, you'll find it in Iowa.

The Mississippi River System has played a key role in the development not only of this region, but of the entire United States. The third largest river in the world, the Mississippi flows from Minnesota to the Gulf of Mexico. In the 1930s, twenty-five locks and dams were built on the Upper Mississippi north of St. Louis, but the river has not been tamed. Walls protect some communities from high water, but many towns still suffer from floods.

When the United States purchased the Louisiana Territory from France in 1803, the size of the young country doubled with the addition of half a billion acres between the Mississippi and the Rockies. The Mississippi has many large tributaries, including the mighty Missouri River. Explorers Lewis and Clark headed west on the Missouri when they began their expedition to learn more about the newly-acquired Louisiana Territory and the Pacific Northwest.

Shortly after the Louisiana Purchase, the United States defeated the British in the War of 1812. After peace was declared, increasing numbers of European immigrants came to America. Many of them traveled the Mississippi in order to settle its shores or the open frontier to the west. Native American Indians had to adapt to the ways of the pioneers, or they were forced to move further west. The spectacular steel arch at the Jefferson Expansion Memorial in St. Louis, Missouri, commemorates the city as the historic gateway to the West.

As settlement expanded, farms replaced the huge herds of buffalo that used to roam the prairie. Today, the Great Plains look like a checkerboard of fertile corn and wheat fields. Much of the grain is loaded onto huge barges that take it down the Mississippi to the port of New Orleans, a lovely Louisiana city that still keeps the flavor of its French past. The city is also noted for its Dixieland jazz and its festive annual Mardi Gras parade.

Before the Civil War, thousands of steamboats carried passengers up and down the Mississippi. Today, steamboats serve as elegant floating hotels for vacationers and gamblers. Mark Twain, from Hannibal, Missouri, was America's most famous river boat pilot and one of the most popular authors. His books described nineteenth century life on the river and the adventures of Tom Sawyer and Huckleberry Finn, characters he created based on his Missouri childhood.

After the Civil War, trains became the fastest, cheapest and most popular form of long-distance transportation. The transcontinental railroad crossed the central states, linking the East with the West.

In the South, Texas is the largest state. Productive oil wells helped make it wealthy. Cities like San Antonio preserve much of the state's Mexican heritage. Texas is a land of wide open spaces ideal for raising cattle. Cowboys are still popular in the thriving city of Dallas--the Dallas Cowboys football team, that is!

Like other parts of America, the central states show tremendous variety.   One famous landmark in the North, Mount Rushmore, is a giant monument carved to honor four of the country's most important Presidents: Lincoln, Roosevelt, Jefferson and Washington. In the South, the Mississippi River carves its own path, nature's example of the freedom cherished in the heart of America.

III. Understand It

A. Enlarging your vocabulary improves your comprehension. Each unit contains a different activity for learning vocabulary. Try each way at least once. As you study new words, repeat the activities that work best for you.

Play "yes/no." Working in groups of three to five students, divide up the task of writing each of this unit's vocabulary words on a slip of paper. Put all the slips in a box or basket.

Without looking in the basket, one person will select a slip. The rest of the group's members may look at the vocabulary list and start asking "yes/no" questions to try to figure out which word has been selected. For example, students might ask, "Is it a verb?" or "Does it relate to farming?" The person with the slip must answer each question "yes" or "no," with no further explanation, until the word has been identified. Take turns drawing slips and answering the questions until all the words have been named.

B. With a partner, take turns asking these questions and answering them in complete sentences.

1. What is the primary use of midwestern land?
2. What are midwesterners known for?
3. What is the nickname for Detroit, and why?
4. What is Wisconsin known for?
5. What is Iowa known for?
6. What is the third largest river in the world?
7. What part of the river has been dammed?
8. From what country did the United States purchase the Louisiana Territory?
9. Name a major tributary of the Mississippi River.
10. What countries fought the War of 1812?
11. What monument commemorates the gateway to the West?
12. What animal used to live on the prairie?
13. What are two crops grown in the Great Plains?
14. How is much of the grain transported?
15. What Louisiana city is famous for its music and its annual parade?
16 Who uses steamboats today?
17. Who was Mark Twain?
18. After the Civil War, what form of long-distance transportation became the most popular?
19. What is the largest state in the South?
20. What rock monument honors four American presidents?

IV. Find It

A. Where am I?

Each student takes a turn giving one clue about a location in the central United States. The rest of the class tries to guess where the student is. For example, one student says, "I am standing by a huge silver arch. Where am I?" The first person to answer "St. Louis" wins.

B. Practice giving directions.

On the board, draw a large circle to represent a compass showing *north, northeast, east, southeast, south, southwest, west* and *northwest*. Take turns having each student name a city or landmark in the central United States. The rest of the class will name and point in the direction they would need to go to reach that spot from St. Louis.

V. Discuss It

Think about the following ideas so that you'll be prepared to talk about them in class.

1. Different regions in the United States have different reputations. For example, generalizations about people who live in the Midwest describe them as friendly and traditional. Does your native country have various sections, each with its own reputation? Are the generalizations accurate?

2. The central United States is primarily agricultural. Contrast the advantages and disadvantages of living in the country or the city. Which do you prefer?

3. Some people object to children reading Mark Twain's novel *The Adventures of Huckleberry Finn* because one of the main characters is named "Nigger Jim." Today, "nigger" is an insulting term for an African-American. Do you think children should be allowed to read historic books that contain language considered offensive today?

4. Does your native country have a major river? What role does the river play in the country's economy?

5. In the United States, wheat is the "staff of life," the basic part of the diet. List at least ten common American foods that contain wheat. Is wheat the main staple in your native country? If so, how is it used? If not, what is the main food, and how is it used?

VI. Use It

The best way to learn English is to use it. Doing these activities will give you lots of practice in English.

1. Most states have nicknames and slogans. For example, Missouri is called the "Show Me State." "Show me" suggests that you need to prove that something is true.   Research the nicknames of at least ten states in the central United States and explain their meaning or significance.

2. Choose a place mentioned in this unit that you would like to visit. Research it. In addition to going to the library and talking with people who have been there, on the internet you might look for a website for the place you are interested in. Then play the role of travel agent trying to persuade the class to visit, too.

3. Research any state in the central United States. What was it called before statehood? When did it become a state? What is its capital? What are its best known industries?   Does it have any famous universities, museums, National Parks or other points of interest? If possible, interview people who live or lived there.

4. Imagine that a friend from your native country is about to arrive in New Orleans. During the flight, your friend will listen to a "talking letter" that you have made. For your friend, record on tape your suggestions about interesting places to see and things to do during a three-month visit in the central United States.

5. Find out about the population in the central United States. Research the ethnic makeup of any large midwestern city, and the history of the ethnic groups who live there.

6. Watch a video of the 1939 film *The Wizard of Oz* and summarize it for your class.

7. Many professional sports teams choose names that relate to their home town. Research the names of at least five teams from the central United States and explain how they reflect the local community.

8. Congratulations! A large company has offered you an excellent job at any of their five locations. To select the location you would like best, compare the various cities' cost of living, population, climate, educational and recreational opportunities. Explain to the class why you would choose to live and work in New Orleans, Dallas, St. Louis, Detroit or Chicago.

9. Read all or part of Mark Twain's *Life on the Mississippi*, *The Adventures of Tom Sawyer*, or *The Adventures of Huckleberry Finn*. Briefly summarize it for the class.

10. Congratulations. You have been asked to decide which President should be added to those honored at Mount Rushmore. The sculptor awaits your decision.

11. Research one of the following topics relating to the central United States so that you can tell the class about it in a brief presentation.

      A. a tribe of American Indians, past or present
      B. the Louisiana Purchase
      C. the Lewis & Clark expedition
      D. the War of 1812
      E. the battle of the Alamo in San Antonio
      F. the steamboat era
      G. nineteenth century pioneers to the West
      H. the Civil War
      I. buffalo
      J. Mark Twain
      K. the transcontinental railroad
      L. Dixieland jazz
      M. Mount Rushmore
      N. the automobile industry in Detroit
      O. dams and locks on the Upper Mississippi River
      P. uses of corn
      Q. the flood of 1993
      R. the St. Louis Arch
      S. Mardi Gras

12. Listen to *The Battle of New Orleans*, a song about Andrew Jackson's victory against the British during the War of 1812. Copy the lyrics, explain their meaning, and lead the class in singing along.

VII. Debate It

Form debate teams that argue *pro* or *con* on the following topics. After listening to the teams' arguments, students in the rest of the class may ask questions of the teams, and then vote *pro* or *con* in secret ballot.

1. To make up for past injustice, every Native American at age eighteen should be given twenty thousand dollars.

2. Within five years, the government should require all new cars sold in the United States to be one hundred percent clean and efficient, causing no pollution.

3. Gambling should be legal throughout the United States.

4. Debate a topic you choose that relates to this unit. State the idea in one sentence so that people can argue pro or con.

VIII. Consider the Proverbs

Guess what each of these sayings means, and give an example that illustrates each one. Be prepared to share it with the class. Does your native language have any of the same proverbs? If so, compare them.

1. If it ain't broke, don't fix it.
2. Make hay while the sun shines.
3. Don't cry over spilled milk.
4. It's like looking for a needle in a haystack.
5. A watched pot never boils.

102

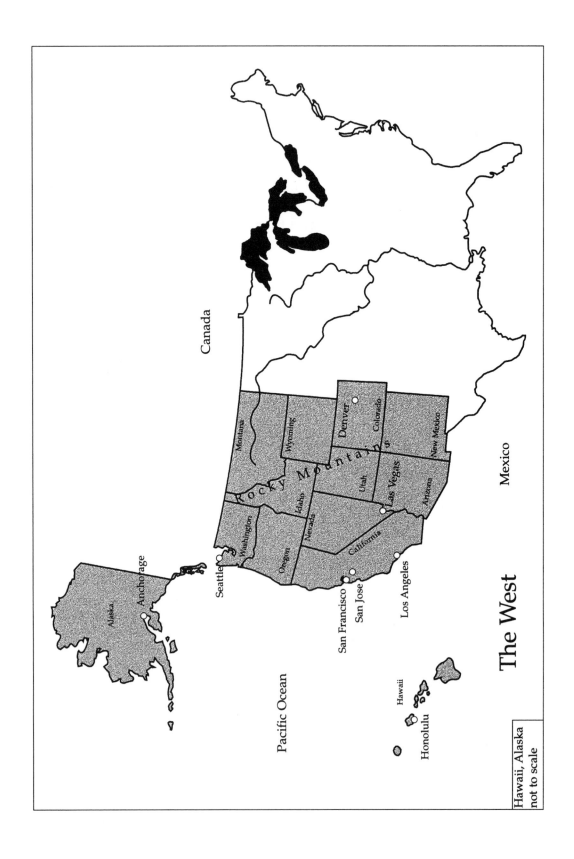

The West

Hawaii, Alaska
not to scale

10
The West
Past & Present

I. Get Ready

A. Before you watch the video, work with a partner to -

- identify eight major cities in the West and the states they're located in.

- identify at least three of the West's geographic features, such as mountains or rivers.

- name any famous historical event that especially affected the western United States.

- pose a question you have about the geography or history of the western United States. If your question is not answered in the video, ask your teacher. Your teacher may tell you the answer, or refer you to the library so you can get the information yourself and share it with the class.

B. To improve your comprehension of the video, review this vocabulary:

diverse - varied
inhabit - to live in (a place)
dwelling - a house
ancestor - a person from whom one is descended

sculpture - a three-dimensional work of art

transform - to change

abound - to occur in great quantities

spires - tall, pointed towers, typically on churches

terrain - landscape

roam - to wander

vast - extensive, very large

mission - a religious settlement whose purpose is to gain new
    members in a foreign land

incredible - amazing; hard to believe

fertile - rich and productive

extinct - died out

thriving - flourishing, prosperous

II. Watch the Video

Watch and listen to the video. During the interview with Californian Malika Mouwattakil, notice her comments about the variety of people, places and activities in the western United States.

After watching the video, read the text below. It matches the narration.

The American West contains scenery as diverse as the people who have inhabited the land.

In the Southwest hundreds of ago years ago, American Indians carved out cliff dwellings in the colorful rock. Today, Navaho guides describe the history of Native American ancestors in the dry, desert lands. Cactus and rock formations look like sculptures decorating the landscape of New Mexico, Arizona and Utah.

The mighty Colorado River carved the biggest canyon in the United States, Arizona's Grand Canyon, through rock layers millions of years old. Built in the 1930s, Hoover Dam on the Colorado River generates electricity that lights much of the West. The glittering signs in Las Vegas, Nevada, make the gambling capital of the United States the city that never sleeps. Upstream on the Colorado River, the Glen Canyon Dam transformed a desert into huge Lake Powell.

National Parks abound in the West. In Utah's Bryce Canyon

National Park, nature carved red, orange and yellow rock into tall spires.   Hikers and riders explore the unusual terrain.   Near Bryce, Zion Canyon National Park is famous for its beautiful sandstone cliffs.

In the state of Colorado, Rocky Mountain National Park is popular with campers and hikers who climb peaks over fourteen thousand feet high.   It's not far from Denver, nicknamed the "Mile High City."   In Wyoming, Yellowstone National Park may be the most famous for its Old Faithful geyser, waterfalls and wildlife.   Bison–sometimes called American buffalo–used to roam in vast herds.   The few buffalo remaining today generally live in national parks.

The era of the cowboys is long past, but Americans preserve the romantic images of cowboys and mountain men.   Cowboy hats and boots are still popular, but today's Americans use horses for recreation.

In the late eighteenth and early nineteenth centuries, the Spanish tried to take control of the land north of Mexico. They established twenty-one missions from Mexico to northern California.   After the Mexican-American War, the Treaty of Guadalupe Hidalgo awarded the United States the land that later became California, Nevada, Utah, New Mexico, Arizona, Texas and parts of Wyoming and Colorado.

Gold was discovered in California in 1848. The next year, the Gold Rush began.   Thousands of '49ers traveled from the East Coast to "get rich quick."   Only a few got rich, but most of them stayed in California. Today, Los Angeles is the largest city in the nation.

California has incredible variety.   The Pacific coast beaches make a sharp contrast with Death Valley, only a few hours' drive from Los Angeles.   Almost three hundred feet below sea level, Death Valley is one of the world's hottest and driest places.

To the north of Death Valley, in the Sierra Nevada Mountains, Yosemite National Park attracts visitors from around the world.   They marvel at the massive granite cliffs, spectacular water falls and lovely landscapes.   Not far from Yosemite, Lake Tahoe is popular for skiing in the winter and sightseeing all year round.

California's fertile soil grows much of the country's fruits and vegetables.   Logging is another major industry, but many redwood forests have been preserved.

The Pacific Coast is lined with picturesque towns, meadows and rugged cliffs.   Surfing is especially popular in Santa Cruz, California.

San Francisco's famous landmarks include Fisherman's Wharf, the

Golden Gate Bridge, cable cars, and Chinatown. Tourism drives the economy of San Francisco, whereas technology drives the San Jose area, nicknamed Silicon Valley for its electronics and computer industries.

Oregon and Washington are sometimes called the Pacific Northwest. Crater Lake National Park in southern Oregon provides an example of an extinct volcano. It contrasts with Mt. St. Helen's, an active volcano in the state of Washington. The defining landmark of the thriving city of Seattle is the space needle tower built for the 1968 World's Fair.

Northwest of Washington, Alaska is nicknamed "The Last Frontier." Fishing villages dot the Alaskan coast, but the population in this vast state is small. Anchorage is the largest city, not far from Mount McKinley, the highest peak in North America. Wilderness, wildlife, snow-capped mountains and glaciers dominate the landscape.

Tourists flock to the Hawaiian Islands. They may visit Pearl Harbor in Honolulu, watch traditional dancing, or lounge on beautiful beaches and enjoy the tropical climate.

Today, adventurers continue to come to the American West, searching for their own pot of gold at the end of the rainbow.

III. Understand It

A. Enlarging your vocabulary improves your comprehension. Each unit contains a different activity for learning vocabulary. Try each way at least once. As you study new words, repeat the activities that work best for you.

Make flash cards. Write the vocabulary word on one side and its meaning on the other. Review the words, saying them and their definitions aloud. Then, work with a partner to test each other.

Randomly select a card from the pile of flash cards. Explain to your partner how you remember that word and its definition. For example,

- Do you have a memory trick you apply to it?
- Do you have a visual image that you connect with the word?
- Can you pair the word with its opposite?

- Do you know the word's rhyme?
- Can you relate the word to a physical activity?

Let's say you're memorizing the word "gamble." "Gamble" is written almost like the word "game," only longer. You might remember that "to gamble" is like playing a long game. Because gambling is a risky game of chance, its opposite might be "playing it safe." "Gamble" rhymes with ramble. If you want to gamble, you could ramble over to Las Vegas. As for a physical activity, as you say the word "gamble" you might pretend to be shaking the dice, pulling the handle of the slot machine, or shuffling a deck of cards--all activities associated with gambling. Cross your fingers for good luck!

B. With a partner, take turns asking these questions and answering them in complete sentences.

1. Who carved cliff dwellings?
2. What are two national parks in Utah?
3. What river carved the Grand Canyon?
4. What dam generates much of the West's electricity?
5. Where is the gambling capital of the United States?
6. What national park is located in Colorado?
7. What is Denver's nickname?
8. Which national park is the most famous?
9. What did the Spanish build in California?
10. What land did the U. S. gain after the Mexican-American War?
11. What did the '49ers want?
12. What city is the nation's largest?
13. What are some famous landmarks in San Francisco?
14. What area is nicknamed "Silicon Valley"?
15. What is an extinct volcano in Oregon?
16. What is an active volcano in Washington?
17. What is Seattle's most famous landmark?
18. What state is known as "The Last Frontier"?
19. What is the highest peak in North America?
20. What may tourists do in Hawaii?

IV. Find It

A. Working with a partner, answer the following questions.

1. What is the biggest mountain range in the western United States?
2. Which ocean borders the west coast?
3. What country is to the north?
4. What country is to the south?
5. What state is made up of islands?

B. Practice giving directions.

On the board, draw a large circle to represent a compass showing *north, northeast, east, southeast, south, southwest, west* a n d *northwest*.

Then take turns having each student name a city or landmark in the western United States. The rest of the class will then name and point in the direction they would need to go to reach that spot from Denver.

V. Discuss It

Think about the following ideas so that you'll be prepared to talk about them in class.

1. In 1849, Horace Greeley wrote in his newspaper *The New York Tribune*, "Go west, young man." The West offered opportunity and adventure. In your native country, does an expression or region represent the feeling of new frontiers or possibilities? Do different parts of your native country have different images? What is the image of the region you are from?

2. List the five states that have Pacific coastline. What effect do you think the ocean has on the people who live near it? In what ways is your native country affected by an ocean or rivers?

3. Twenty-five percent of California's residents were not born in the United States. What do you think attracts them to this state? What do you think is their impact on California?

4. Immigrants from all over the world come to the United States. Sometimes cultural misunderstandings occur when people from different cultures interact. Have you experienced any situations in which a misunderstanding—humorous or serious—occurred due to differences in culture?

5. Before you came to the United States, what did you expect life in America to be like? Compare what you expected and what you have found.

6. California earthquakes cause significant damage to property, and sometimes they kill and injure many people. Would you live in California, or would fear of earthquakes make you avoid the state? Do earthquakes, hurricanes or tornadoes occur in your native country?

7. Tradition and history define much of the image of the eastern United States, while the West glorifies youth and change. Where would you feel most comfortable living? Is tradition or change valued more in your native country?

VI. Use It

The best way to learn English is to use it. Doing these activities will give you lots of practice in English.
When you finish your research, share your findings with the class.

1. Contact AMTRAK and get the train schedule and cost for a trip you imagine that would take you to at least four of the places mentioned in this unit.

2. Contact an airline or travel agent and get the schedule and cost for a trip you imagine that would take you to at least four of the places mentioned in this unit.

3. Contact a car rental agency and find out the cost for a trip you imagine that would take you to at least four of the places mentioned in this unit.

4. Contact a bus line and find out the cost for a trip you imagine that would take you to at least four of the places mentioned in this unit.

5. Choose a place mentioned in this unit that you would like to visit. Research it. In addition to going to the library and talking with people who have been there, on the internet you might look for a website with information about the place you are interested in.

   Then play the role of travel agent trying to persuade the class to visit, too.

6. Research one of the following topics relating to the West.
   A. a tribe of American Indians, past or present
   B. California missions
   C. Mormon pioneers
   D. the Mexican-American War
   E. the Gold Rush
   F. the Pony Express
   G. building the transcontinental railroad
   H. the National Park system
   I. building Hoover Dam
   J. gambling in Nevada
   K. smog: its causes and consequences
   L. the role of Pearl Harbor in World War II
   M. the history of Disneyland
   N. the Hollywood film industry
   O. the Alaskan oil pipeline
   P. "Silicon Valley"
   Q. earthquakes
   R. wildfires

    S.   volcanoes

    T.   redwood trees

    U. endangered species

    V.   the logging industry, past & present

7. Bring history to life! Research an event mentioned in this unit. Alone or with classmates, present a mini-play dramatizing the history you studied.   In character, explain what "you" did and why.

8. Research any state in the western United States. What was it called before statehood? When did it become a state? What is its capital? What are its major industries? Does it have any famous universities, museums, National Parks or other points of interest? If possible, interview people who live or lived there.

9. Imagine that a friend from your native country is about to arrive in Los Angeles. During the flight, your friend will listen to a "talking letter" that you have made. For your friend, record on tape your suggestions about interesting places to see and things to do during a three-month visit in the West.

10. Most states have nicknames and slogans. For example, California is called the "Golden State." Research the nicknames of at least eight states in the West and explain their meaning or significance.

11. California is the most populous state in the nation, and Wyoming is the least. Why? Research the states' climates, industries and educational opportunities, and then answer the question.

12. Find out about the population in the West. Research the ethnic makeup of any large western city, and the history of the ethnic groups who live there.

13. Congratulations! A large company has offered you an excellent job at any of their five locations. To select the location you would like best, compare the various cities' cost of living, population, climate, educational and recreational opportunities. Explain to the class why

you would choose to live and work in Los Angeles, San Francisco, Seattle, Anchorage or Honolulu.

VII.   Debate It

Form debate teams that argue *pro* or *con* on the following topics. After listening to the teams' arguments, students in the rest of the class may ask questions of the teams, and then vote *pro* or *con* in secret ballot.

1. ? should become the fifty-first state.

2. Opening the U. S. - Mexican border for free trade and immigration would benefit both countries.

3. Space is today's last frontier, and the United States should make its exploration a top priority.

4. Debate a topic you choose that relates to this unit. State the idea in one sentence so that people can argue pro or con.

VIII.   Consider the Proverbs

Guess what each of these sayings means. Then, give an example that illustrates each one. Be prepared to explain it to the class. Does your native language have any of the same proverbs? If so, compare them.

1. One bad apple can ruin the whole barrel.
2. No pain, no gain.
3. All that glitters is not gold.
4. Some people can't see the forest for the trees.
5. A rolling stone gathers no moss.

11

Holidays

January - June

I. Get Ready

A. Before you watch the video, work with a partner to -

- list all the American holidays you can think of between January and June.

- note any holidays during the first half of the year that are also celebrated in your native country.

- pose a question you have about an American holiday between January and June. If your question is not answered in the video, ask your teacher. Your teacher may tell you the answer, or refer you to an information source so you can get the answer yourself and share it with the class.

B. To improve your comprehension of the video, review this vocabulary:

racism - unfair treatment because of a person's skin color
inspiration - admirable example
portrait - a picture of a person
fiddling - playing traditional folk music on the violin
prank - a trick or joke

think twice - to be sure

symbolic - representing something

bless - to say a short prayer about a person or thing

lunar - relating to the moon

crucified - killed by being nailed to a cross

eternal - lasting forever

dye - to change a color

Mardi Gras - "Fat Tuesday," the day before Lent, which is the season
    preceding Easter

flock - come in large numbers

elaborate - large and detailed

signifies - represents

II.   Watch the Video

Watch and listen to the video. During the interview with Katie Kendall-Weed, notice her comments about the fun of maintaining Irish fiddling traditions on St. Patrick's Day.

After watching the video, read the text below. It matches the narration.

Martin Luther King was a civil rights leader famous for his peaceful efforts to end racism. He was born January 15, 1929, and his birthday is celebrated the third Monday in January. King was killed in 1968, but he is well remembered for his inspiration and leadership in the struggle of African-Americans to gain equal rights.

Traditional dragons, parades, sweet oranges and red money envelopes are part of the Chinese New Year celebration enjoyed by some Asian-Americans in late January or early February.

On Valentine's Day, many people give candy and flowers to their family, special friends and sweethearts. They may send Valentine's cards that they buy or that they make themselves. Red, pink and white are the typical colors. At most schools, the children have a party and exchange Valentines with their classmates. The date, February 14, marks the birth of the Christian St. Valentine, but in America the holiday is not celebrated as a religious event.

Abraham Lincoln led the United States through the Civil War from

1861 to 1865. He is probably best known for preserving the Union, or keeping the country united, and for freeing the slaves. The Lincoln Memorial in Washington D.C. is a popular tourist attraction. Presidents' Day, the third Monday in February, is a legal holiday in honor of the birthdays of Abraham Lincoln as well as George Washington.

Called "The Father of our Country," Washington was the first President of the United States. A famous portrait of Washington hangs in the White House, the home of the President. The tall Washington Monument, near the Potomac River, is one of Washington D.C.'s best-known landmarks.

On March 17, many people celebrate St. Patrick's Day by wearing green, drinking beer and Irish whiskey, and enjoying Irish fiddling. Bars are usually crowded on St. Patty's day.

If someone says "April Fools!" you can expect a prank. You'd better think twice before you believe everything you see and hear on April 1, for that's April Fool's Day.

Passover, an important Jewish holiday in the spring, celebrates the Jews passing from slavery in Egypt into freedom. Symbolic food is prepared for the Seder, the big Passover dinner. The mother blesses the candles, and a prayer is said over the wine. The family reads the story of Passover and enjoys a delicious meal together.

Easter is a Christian holiday celebrated on a Sunday in the spring. Like Passover, its date varies because it is determined by the lunar calendar. The Friday before Easter Sunday, called Good Friday, Jesus Christ was crucified. According to the Bible, three days later Jesus rose to heaven and began his eternal life. Symbols of birth are common at Easter, such as chicks, ducklings, eggs and rabbits. Dyeing Easter eggs is a popular tradition. So are Easter egg hunts in which kids fill their baskets with colorful eggs. The Easter Bunny leaves candy for the children. Churches are crowded on Easter Sunday. After the service, many families enjoy a big Easter dinner.

New Orleans is famous for its Mardi Gras parade six and a half weeks before Easter. Merrymakers flock to the carnival and cheer the elaborate floats.

In California and the Southwest, May 5 is celebrated as "Cinco de Mayo." The Mexican-American holiday features music, parades and dancing.

On Mother's Day, the second Sunday in May, many children give their Mom flowers, candy, a card or just a hug that says "I love you." Restaurants are always crowded on Mother's Day. This is one time mothers rarely do the cooking.

Memorial Day, the last Monday in May, is a legal holiday in honor of all those who have been killed in wars. Many people display the American flag, nicknamed the Stars and Stripes. Cities and towns organize parades, and Memorial Day barbecues are popular. This three-day weekend signifies the beginning of summer.

The third Sunday in June is Father's Day. Then it's Dad's turn to get presents, cards and appreciation.

III.   Understand It

A. Enlarging your vocabulary improves your comprehension. Each unit contains a different activity for learning vocabulary. Try each way at least once. As you study new words, repeat the activities that work best for you.

Play bingo. To prepare, students should each draw a grid consisting of twenty-five equal squares (five across and five down). Write twenty-five of the items listed below, one in each square, in random order. Each student's card will be unique.

inspiration	King	Washington
portrait	Easter	Passover
fiddling	Lincoln	Mother's Day
think twice	Father's Day	Memorial Day
prank	Valentine's Day	bless
crucified	eternal	dye
Mardi Gras	flock	symbolic
Cinco de Mayo	signifies	lunar
eggs	bunnies	ducklings
fool	hunt	church

To begin the game, the instructor or a student reads a definition, a date, or any information that students should connect with one of the words or names listed above. Students put a check on their grids by each item described. The first to have five checks in a row—horizontally, vertically, or diagonally—wins!

B. With a partner, take turns asking these questions and answering them in complete sentences.

1. What is Martin Luther King famous for?
2. When is King's birthday celebrated?
3. What things are typical of Chinese New Year?
4. When is Valentine's Day?
5. What do people do on Valentine's Day?
6. During what war was Abraham Lincoln President?
7. What were his two greatest accomplishments?
8. What is George Washington called?
9. How do many people celebrate St. Patrick's Day?
10. What's the day for pranks and jokes?
11. What Jewish holiday is celebrated in the Spring?
12. What does Passover celebrate?
13. On what day was Jesus Christ crucified?
14. What are the common symbols of birth at Easter?
15. What does the Easter Bunny do?
16. What holiday is New Orleans famous for?
17. What holiday is celebrated by many Mexican-Americans?
18. When is Mother's Day?
19. Who is honored on Memorial Day?
20. When is Father's Day?

IV. Know What to Celebrate

Working in pairs, fill in the name of the person or holiday described:

1. leader of   3rd Monday in   _____
   African-Americans   January

2. love, hearts, candy February 14   _____

3. Father of Our Country   3rd Monday in February   _____

4. New Orleans   6 weeks before Easter   _____

5. green, Irish   March 17   _____

6. jokes, pranks   April 1   _____

7. Mexican parades   May 5   _____

8. Mom   2nd Sunday in May   _____

9. flags, picnics   last Monday in May   _____

10. Dad   3rd Sunday in June   _____

V. Discuss It

Think about the following ideas so that you'll be prepared to talk about them in class.

1. Many of America's legal holidays honor military and political heroes. Does this seem right and normal to you, or do you think other types of heroes (for example, famous doctors and scientists) would be more inspiring? What makes a person a "hero"?

2. Both Passover and Easter celebrate new life. Does your native country have a similar holiday at the beginning of the growing season? Compare that holiday with Easter or Passover in the United States.

3. Abraham Lincoln was born into a poor family. By studying and working hard, he became a lawyer, a politician, and finally President. Do you think a poor person could achieve such success today?

4. Although holidays vary from one country to another, all countries have annual traditions. What functions do they serve in unifying a

country and culture? Consider the role of holidays in your native country as well as in the United States.

5. On Memorial Day it is very common for cities and towns to organize parades. In your native country, is a holiday celebrated with parades? Compare it to Memorial Day.

6. Although it is common to refer to "African-Americans" or "Asian-Americans," most citizens of Caucasian background simply call themselves "Americans." Do you think they should be called "Caucasian-Americans"? Or would it be better to call all citizens "Americans"?

7. Does racism exist in your native country? Explain the situation to the rest of the class.

8. On Mother's Day and Father's Day, children often show their appreciation to their parents by giving them gifts, preparing a special breakfast or taking them out to dinner. Compare the attitudes of children toward their parents in your native country with the attitudes in America.

9. Does your native country have regions that celebrate their own local holidays? If so, describe one of them to the class.

10. Most successful people are risk-takers. Sometimes they fail, but they learn from their mistakes and eventually succeed. Can you name any successful people who have experienced failures? Can you think of any examples in your own life when you learned something from a failure?

VII. Use It

The best way to learn English is to use it. Doing these activities will give you lots of practice in English.

1. Research the history of Valentine's Day, April Fools' Day, Mardi

Gras, St. Patrick's Day or Cinco de Mayo. Explain to the class what you learned.

2. "Mardi Gras" is a French expression meaning "Fat Tuesday," and "Cinco de Mayo" is Spanish for "fifth of May." English contains many words and expressions borrowed from other languages. Using a large dictionary, research the history of any five words mentioned in this unit. Explain their origin.

3. Study the life of one of the men whose birthday is celebrated in January or February (King, Lincoln or Washington). In a five-minute speech, explain that person's importance in American history; or "become" that person and describe your life.

4. No American holiday honors a particular woman. Research the contributions of an outstanding American woman and share your findings with the class in a three-minute presentation. While you are speaking, classmates will take notes about your information and ask any questions they may have. Then, ask for a volunteer to give a thirty-second summary of your speech. Finally, your instructor may give a quiz about the information presented. Students may use their notes. You are not limited to the following suggestions:

- Sacajawea (?1787 - ?1812) frontier guide
- Lucretia Mott (1793 - 1880) women's rights activist
- Sojourner Truth (?1797 - 1883) abolitionist and women's rights activist
- Harriet Beecher Stowe (1811 - 1896) author
- Elizabeth Cady Stanton (1815 - 1902) women's rights activist
- Susan B. Anthony (1820 - 1906) women's rights activist
- Harriet Tubman (?1820-1913) abolitionist
- Clara Barton (1821 - 1912) founder of the American Red Cross
- Nellie Bly (1864 - 1922) journalist
- Mother Jones (1830-1930) labor leader
- Margaret Sanger (1883 - 1966) women's health activist

- Eleanor Roosevelt (1884 - 1962) political leader
- Georgia O'Keeffe (1887 - 1986) painter
- Amelia Earhart (1897 - 1937) pilot
- Rosa Parks (1913 -   ) civil rights activist
- Ella Fitzgerald (1917 - 1996) jazz singer
- Betty Friedan (1921 -) women's rights activist
- Maya Angelou (1928 -) author
- Gloria Steinem (1934 -) women's rights activist
- Shannon Lucid (1943 -) astronaut
- Alice Walker (1944 -) author

5. Ask your instructor to recommend videos relating to the people or holidays discussed in this unit. For example, your library may have a copy of the Public Broadcasting System's documentary about the Civil Rights movement called *Eyes on the Prize*. After viewing one of the segments, prepare a brief summary for the class.

6. Play the game called *Who Am I?* Each student will give five clues (pieces of information) about a famous American politician, hero, artist, author, scientist, etc. Each clue should be a short statement beginning with "I am" or "I was." Every statement should be more specific than the one given before it. After all five clues have been given, the class guesses who the famous person is (or was). For example, the student giving the clues says:

> " 1. I was a 19th Century woman.
>   2. I was a teacher.
>   3. I lectured against slavery.
>   4. I led the movement for women's right to vote.
>   5. I was pictured on the silver dollar.
>   Who was I?"

The class answers: "Susan B. Anthony"

7. Lead the class in singing *Let My People Go*. The words and music are in the Appendix.

VIII.   Debate It

Form debate teams that argue *pro* or *con* on the following topics. After listening to the teams' arguments, students in the rest of the class may ask questions of the teams, and then vote *pro* or *con* in secret ballot.

1. Racial equality can be achieved in the United States.

2. Celebrating ethnic holidays such as St. Patrick's Day and Cinco de Mayo encourages an appreciation of immigrants from many lands.

3. Mothers and fathers should share equally in parenting their children.

4. Debate a topic you choose that relates to this unit. State the idea in one sentence so that people can argue pro or con.

IX.   Consider the Proverbs

Guess what each of these sayings means. Then, give an example that illustrates each one. Be prepared to share it with the class. Does your native language have any of the same proverbs? If so, compare them.

1. Seeing is believing.
2. Look before you leap.
3. Which came first, the chicken or the egg?
4. Honesty is the best policy.
5. "You can fool all the people some of the time, and some of the people all the time, but you can not fool all the people all of the time."
Abraham Lincoln

12

Holidays

July - November

I. Get Ready

A. Before you watch the video, work with a partner to -

- list all the American holidays between July and November that you can think of .

- name at least one tradition associated with one of those holidays.

- pose a question you have about an American holiday between July and November. If your question is not answered in the video, ask your teacher. Your teacher may tell you the answer, or refer you to an information source so you can get the answer yourself and share it with the class.

B. To improve your comprehension of the video, review this vocabulary:

patriotism - loyalty to one's country
jammed - crowded
ancient - very old
superstition - a belief not based on fact
witch - a woman with magical powers, usually considered evil,
ghost - a person's soul

skeleton - bones
on the loose - wild, roaming around
carve - to cut with a knife
Jack O'Lantern - a carved pumpkin
veterans - people with experience in a particular job or activity
harvest - crops gathered at the end of the growing season
gravy - a sauce poured over meat

II. Watch the Video

Watch and listen to the video. During the interview with the Halloween trick or treaters, notice their excitement about wearing costumes, visiting houses and getting candy.

After watching the video, read the text below. It matches the narration.

The 4th of July, Independence Day, celebrates the birth of the United States in 1776. To show their patriotism, some people display American flags. Summer sunshine is perfect for 4th of July fairs, picnics, barbecues and parades. After the sun sets, it's time for the fireworks.

Labor Day, the first Monday in September, is a day off in honor of all the working people in America. It's the last three-day weekend before school begins in the fall. Highways and parking lots are jammed. So are hotels, motels, parks and campgrounds as families enjoy the last holiday of the summer.

Christopher Columbus, an Italian ship captain hired by Spain, reached America in 1492. Government offices, banks and many schools close for Columbus Day, the second Monday in October. After Columbus's voyage, many Europeans migrated to the New World, changing forever the lives of the American Indians.

Halloween is a traditional holiday celebrated October 31. According to ancient superstitions, Halloween was the night that witches could fly, and ghosts and skeletons were on the loose. If a black cat crosses your path, watch out, because that brings bad luck!

To get ready for Halloween, kids choose bright orange pumpkins. Then they carve them into smiling Jack O'Lanterns. Wearing

Halloween costumes is lots of fun.

On Halloween night kids go "trick or treating." Groups of children walk from house to house. When the front door opens, the kids yell "Trick or treat!" They are usually given fruit or candy.

Veterans Day, November 11, is a legal holiday honoring all those who have served in the armed forces. Veterans often organize parades and memorial services on this day to remember their past military duty for their country.

The fourth Thursday in November is Thanksgiving. The Thanksgiving tradition began in 1621 with the Pilgrims, English settlers in America. They celebrated a successful harvest. Today, schools and many businesses close for the four-day weekend.

Thanksgiving is a time for families and friends to come home, enjoy being together and to appreciate all the good things in their lives. On Thanksgiving Day, people greet each other warmly. They eat, drink, and catch up with the news. They may phone family members who don't make it home for the holiday. "We miss you!"

Turkey is the traditional food at Thanksgiving. The big bird roasts for hours. The gravy to be poured on top is delicious. When the cooking is done, the turkey is carved, and the table is set, it's finally time for dinner. The huge meal ends with pumpkin pie.

Thanksgiving marks the end of fall and makes us think about what comes next—the Christmas Season.

III. Understand It

A. Enlarging your vocabulary improves your comprehension. Each unit contains a different activity for learning vocabulary. Try each way at least once. As you study new words, repeat the activities that work best for you.

Working in teams, select the word in these groups that does not belong with the others. Be prepared to explain the reason for your choices.

a) witch ghost patriotism skeleton

b) Pilgrims turkey Jack O'Lantern gravy

c) fireworks patriotism carve flags

d) carve ancient turkey harvest

e) red white blue orange

B. With a partner, take turns asking these questions and answering them in complete sentences.

1. What does the 4th of July celebrate?
2. What are some popular activities on the 4th of July?
3. What three-day weekend comes at the end of summer?
4. When did Columbus reach America?
5. According to superstitions, what is special about Halloween night?
6. What brings bad luck?
7   What do kids do with pumpkins at Halloween?
8. What do kids do when they go "trick or treating"?
9. Who does Veterans Day honor?
10. What are some traditional Veterans Day activities?
11. When did the Thanksgiving tradition begin?
12. What is the main part of Thanksgiving dinner?
13. What is served for dessert?

C. Fill in the blanks using the words in the list below. They will not all be used.

veterans	carve
Pilgrims	skeleton
witch	harvest
ghost	Jack O'Lantern
gravy	patriotism
superstitions	ancient
trick or treat	veterans

Some Americans show their _____ by

flying a flag on the 4th of July.

According to very old _____, on Halloween night the dead come alive. When it's time to trick or treat, kids wear costumes, such as a _____, _____ or _____. Using a knife, they may _____ a pumpkin into a _____.

The Thanksgiving tradition began in the seventeenth century when the _____ celebrated their first successful _____. For dinner, the roasted turkey is covered with thick _____. The big meal ends with pumpkin pie.

IV. Practice It

A. Write the letter of the holiday listed on the right which is celebrated on the date listed on the left.

1. _____4th of July   A   Columbus Day

2. _____first Monday in September   B. Veterans Day

3. _____fourth Thursday in November   C. Independence Day

4. _____November 11   D. Labor Day

5. _____October 31   E. Halloween

6. _____second Monday in October   F. Thanksgiving

B. Write the letter of the holiday listed on the right which best matches the ideas listed on the left. Some of them will be used more than once.

1. _____ turkey

2. _____ "trick or treat"

3. _____ fireworks   A. 4th of July

4. _____ four-day weekend   B. Labor Day

5. _____ Jack O' Lanterns   C. Columbus Day

6. _____ independence   D. Halloween

7. _____ end of summer   E. Veterans Day

8. _____ military honor   F. Thanksgiving

9. _____ witches, black cats

10. _____ 1492

V. Recite It

A. Twist Your Tongue

A "tongue twister" makes little sense, but it is fun to say because of its repeated sounds. Try saying each of these tongue twisters three times fast. Make up your own, using a sound that you need to practice pronouncing.

1. How much wood could a woodchuck chuck if a woodchuck could chuck wood?

2. Peter Piper picked a peck of pickled peppers. How many pecks of pickled peppers did Peter Piper pick?

3. She sells sea shells by the sea shore.

B. Recite a Limerick

Practicing the rhythm of English improves your pronunciation. One way to do this is to recite a limerick—a short, often humorous poem with a strong rhythm pattern. Pause at the end of each of the first two lines. You may want to clap your hands or tap on a desk to keep the rhythm steady.

> (tap)   (tap)   (tap)   (tap)
> da DAH da da DAH da da DAH
> da DAH da da DAH da da DAH
> da DAH da da DAH da
> da DAH da da DAH da
> da DAH da da DAH da da DAH

Emphasize the rhythm as you read this limerick, adapted from the poetry of Leonard Stonehill:

> Who's here? It's a Halloween witch,
> But night time's created a hitch.
> She meets with her coven,
> It's dark as an oven
> And hard to tell which witch is which!

Find a collection of limericks at the library. Memorize one, and recite it for the class. Also, you might try composing your own.

VI. Discuss It

Think about the following ideas so that you'll be prepared to talk about them in class.

1. Does your native country have an independence day holiday? If so, compare it to the celebrations on the American 4th of July.

2. Do people in your native country celebrate any holiday by wearing costumes? If so, describe the holiday.

3. Does your native country have an annual celebration relating to witchcraft or spirits of the dead? If so, compare it to Halloween.

4. In your native country, is there a celebration at the end of the harvest season? If so, compare it to Thanksgiving.

5. The 4th of July is a patriotic holiday. What does patriotism mean to you? Can immigrants be loyal to both their native country and the United States, too?

6. Most Americans eat meat, but vegetarianism has been increasing. Do you eat meat? Why or why not? Is vegetarianism common in your native country?

7. Explain any holiday celebrated between July and November in your native country.

VII. Use It

The best way to learn English is to use it. Doing these activities will give you lots of practice in English.

1. Indians lived in America for hundreds of years before Europeans came. When the Pilgrims landed in New England, they probably would not have survived without the help of the Native Americans. Research an American Indian tribe in your area. Report to the class what you found out.

2. Organize a potluck Thanksgiving dinner. A "potluck" means everyone brings something to eat. For example, one person brings a pumpkin pie, another brings something to drink, another brings sweet potatoes, etc. Probably you will want several people to work together stuffing the turkey and roasting it. If you're not sure about the American style of cooking, you'd better use a cookbook.

3. Ask at least five people if they believe in any of the following superstitions familiar to many Americans, and share your findings with the class.

These bring bad luck:

- a black cat crosses your path

- you walk under a ladder

- you open an umbrella indoors

- you put a hat on a bed

- the number thirteen

- Friday the 13th

- breaking a mirror (That causes seven years of bad luck.)

These bring good luck:

- the number seven

- crossing your fingers

- knocking on wood (That causes good luck to continue.)

4. Do you believe in any of the superstitions listed above? Can you think of any other superstitions from your native country?

5. Research the history of any American holiday celebrated between July and November and share your findings with the class.

6. Research the origin of Jack O' Lanterns. If pumpkins are available, carve your own Jack O'Lantern and show it to the class.

7. Make a tape. Record your own informal description of an American holiday as if you were explaining it to someone new to the United States. You may use notes, but do not read your explanation word for word. Exchange tapes with your classmates. At the end of your classmate's tape, record at least three positive comments about it.

8. Lead the class in singing *The Star-Spangled Banner* and *Over the River*. The words and music are in the Appendix.

VIII. Debate It

Form debate teams that argue *pro* or *con* on the following topics. After listening to the teams' arguments, students in the rest of the class may ask questions of the teams, and then vote *pro* or *con* in secret ballot.

1. "Freedom" in the United States should include the right to burn the American flag.

2. Columbus Day should be replaced by a holiday honoring American Indians.

3. Being loyal to your country means you always support it.

4. Debate a topic you choose that relates to this unit. State the idea in one sentence so that people can argue pro or con.

IX. Consider the Proverbs

Guess what each of these sayings means. Then, give an example that illustrates each one. Be prepared to share it with the class. Does your native language have any of the same proverbs? If so, compare them.

1. When in Rome, do as the Romans do.
2. One man's meat is another man's poison.
3. Too many cooks spoil the broth.
4. Necessity is the mother of invention.
5. Beauty is in the eye of the beholder.

13

The Holiday Season

I. Get Ready

A. Before you watch the video, work with a partner to -

- list as many words as you can that are associated with Christmas.

- list any tradition you can think of relating to New Year's celebrations in America.

- name any holidays you can think of that have been created within your lifetime.

- write two questions you have about the American holiday season.

B. To improve your comprehension of the video, review this vocabulary:

wreath - a circle of evergreen branches made for decoration
untangle - to straighten, organize
ornament - a decoration for a Christmas tree
stocking - a long sock
carol - a Christmas song
menorah - a Jewish symbolic candle holder
champagne - sparkling white wine

toast - expressing good wishes just before taking a drink
resolution - a promise to make an improvement in one's life

II. Watch the Video

Watch and listen to the video. During the interview with Santa Claus, notice his emphasis on the fun of Christmas.

After watching the video, read the text below. It matches the narration.

Christmas, December 25, is the biggest holiday of the year. Many people decorate their homes with brightly colored lights, greetings, wreaths and red bows. Towns may put lights on a tall pine tree in the park, and if the weather is mild, they may hold a Christmas parade.

The Christmas season brings wishes for peace and happiness. It also brings lots of people to stores to buy presents for their families and friends. Many stores do one-half of the whole year's business during the month before Christmas. Red and green, the traditional Christmas colors, are everywhere.

At shopping malls, many kids sit on Santa's lap and tell him what they want for Christmas. Children believe that Santa leaves his home at the North Pole on Christmas Eve. He flies through the air in his sleigh pulled by reindeer. Santa lands on each roof and slides down the chimney to deliver the gifts.

Many people send greeting cards and gifts through the mail. This is the busiest time of year for the postal service.

One of the most popular Christmas traditions is getting a Christmas tree. You can buy one already cut, or you can cut your own at a Christmas tree farm. To cut your own, you select the pine tree that looks just right to you. Then cut it and load it into your truck or car to take home.

Decorating the tree is lots of fun. First, untangle the Christmas tree lights that have been stored away all year. Then, bring out the ornaments and put them on the tree. Wrapping Christmas presents can be a big job, but the decorated tree surrounded by colorfully wrapped gifts makes a beautiful sight.

Over the holidays, there are many parties, both formal and

informal. Sometimes Santa Claus and Mrs. Santa Claus make a visit, much to the children's delight. Many families live far apart, so telephones keep busy as relatives call to wish each other Merry Christmas.

One Christmas tradition is hanging stockings up on the fireplace. Santa fills them with presents. Some families leave cookies for Santa to enjoy. No wonder he's so fat!

Many people go to church on Christmas eve or early Christmas morning. The holiday celebrates the birth of Jesus Christ two thousand years ago. Singing Christmas carols is usually part of the service.

On the morning of December 25th, it's time to open the presents. That's the most exciting part of Christmas.

After the presents have been opened, everybody's ready for a big Christmas dinner. The kids may make cookies. After the preparations in the kitchen are done, the table is set, and dinner is served. Children who were too excited to fall asleep on Christmas Eve usually dose off exhausted at the end of Christmas day.

Schools are out for vacation the week between Christmas and New Year's, so there's plenty of time for the children to have fun with their new toys.

Some African-Americans celebrate Kwanzaa, a holiday created in 1966. They light a different candle each day between December 26 and January 1 to represent unity, self-determination, collective work and responsibility, cooperative economics, purpose, creativity and faith.

"Shalom!" is a Hebrew greeting that means "Peace!" Jewish Hanukkah is an eight-day festival celebrated during the holiday season. The family lights the menorah to honor the Jews' defeat of the Romans in 165 B.C. The dreydl is a toy used in a gambling game at Hanukkah. The winner usually gets candy, nuts and fruit.

The most famous night for parties is December 31, New Year's Eve. Party-goers open the champagne and make a toast to the New Year. Just before midnight, many people turn on the TV to see the countdown at Times Square in New York City. When the red apple drops, it's 12:00. People wish each other "Happy New Year" and sing the traditional *Auld Lang Syne*. Drinking is common all year, and especially at New Year's Eve celebrations. Drunk drivers are a serious problem.

January 1, New Year's Day, is quiet compared to the night before.

Most people stay home and watch the football games and parades on TV. Some people make New Year's resolutions, but the promises are often forgotten.

III. Understand It

A. Enlarging your vocabulary improves your comprehension. Each unit contains a different activity for learning vocabulary. Try each way at least once. As you study new words, repeat the activities that work best for you.

In the spirit of the holidays, give each other new words that can be used during the holiday season and throughout the new year. Have each student select a word from the vocabulary list and then show the class at least one effective way to remember the word and its meaning. Use your imagination! Each student's turn ends when the whole class can easily repeat the word and its meaning.

B. With a partner, take turns asking these questions and answering them in complete sentences.

1. How are homes decorated at Christmas?
2. What are the traditional Christmas colors?
3. Where do kids see Santa Claus?
4. Where does Santa live?
5. How does Santa Claus travel?
6. How does he bring the presents into each home?
7. Why is Christmas the busiest time for the postal service?
8. What are two ways of getting a Christmas tree?
9. What do people put on trees to decorate them?
10. Where are the stockings hung?
11. When do many people go to church?
12. What does Christmas celebrate?
13. What's the most exciting part of Christmas?
14. When is school on vacation?
15. What is the new African-American holiday?
16. What is "Shalom"?

17. What does Hanukkah celebrate?
18. What night is most famous for parties?
19. What do many people do on New Year's Day?
20. What usually happens to New Year's resolutions?

IV. Practice It

A. Fill in the blanks using the words in the list below.

chimney	reindeer
carols	Santa Claus
gifts	sleigh
greeting cards	stockings
ornaments	tree
colorful	wrapped

After Thanksgiving, people start buying _____ for their

families and friends.   They send_____to many

people. _____lights decorate homes and trees.

When Christmas is not far off, the children hang_____

by the fireplace. The family brings home a _____

which everyone helps to decorate with_____.

The _____ presents go under the tree. On Christmas

Eve, many people sing_____. After the children

go to sleep, _____leaves the North

Pole. He drives his_____pulled by

_____. At each house, he slides down

the_____and delivers gifts to all the children.

V. Say It Right

"The "t" and "th" sounds are easy to confuse. To practice them, create a story about "who bought what."

First, have students get into groups of three or four. Give each group ten blank cards. On each card that one group has, write odd numbers, starting with 1. On each card that another group has, write even numbers starting with 2.

Groups with odd-numbered cards should write names of people that include the "t" or "th" sound, such as "Tom" or "Beth," one name on each card. Groups with even-numbered cards should write names of foods, objects or presents that include the /t/ or /th/ sound, such as "tomatoes" and "thread."

Then, line up the cards by number. Aloud, read about who bought what. Follow this format:

Tom [card 1] bought *tomatoes* [card 2] at the store.

Beth [card 3] bought *thread*[card 4] at the store.

For more practice, continue to "shop," pairing sounds such as *f/p, s/sh, v/b*, and *r/l*.

VI. Discuss It

Think about the following ideas so that you'll be prepared to talk about them in class.

1. Are any of the Christmas traditions in your native country different from those in America? Explain.

2. If you don't celebrate Christmas, describe your biggest holiday. How does it compare with Christmas in America?

3. Do you or others in your native country celebrate Hannukah? If so, compare it with the American tradition.

4. Compare the New Year's celebration in your native country with the American tradition.

5. Do you think Christmas in the United States shows a generous spirit of giving and sharing, or is there too much attention on spending money and buying things? Do Americans generally seem more materialistic than people are in your native country?

6. As we grow older, sometimes our attitudes change. Think of a tradition you have celebrated for many years. Has your attitude toward it changed? Explain.

7. Kwanzaa was created to promote African-American unity and pride. Do you think the holiday is a good idea, or does it add to the feeling of separation between the races in the United States?

8. If you could add a holiday, what would it be? Why?

9. Congratulations. You have been selected to star in a Christmas TV show called "Jack and Jill." In pairs, practice your parts. Volunteers may wish to present the scene to the whole class.

The director tells Jack:
> In your own words, show how much you dislike Christmas. You hate the traffic, crowded stores, and feeling that you have to spend too much money buying presents. Create your own examples as you make your character come to life!

The director tells Jill:
> In your own words, show how much you like Christmas. You love the childhood memories of exciting Christmas mornings, making presents for family members, and enjoying holiday parties. Create your own examples as you make your character come to life!

VII. Use It

The best way to learn English is to use it. Doing these activities will give you lots of practice in English.

1. Research the history of Kwanzaa, and share your findings with the

class.

2. Research the history of Christmas trees in the United States, and share your findings with the class.

3. Research the history and meaning of Hanukkah.

4. Sing a Christmas carol in English, and tell the class about its composer.

5. List five resolutions you would like to make. You may be serious or humorous.

6. Interview people about their New Year's resolutions. Report to the class what you found out.

7. Watch a video of a classic Christmas movie such as *Miracle on 34th Street* or *A Christmas Carol*. In a brief presentation, summarize the story for your classmates.

8. Organize a Christmas party. You might plan food, beverages, music, decorations, invitations, games, etc.

9. Organize a gift or greeting card exchange. Have each student write his or her name on a slip of paper, and put all the slips in a bag. Limit the value of the gifts or cards so that everyone can afford to participate. Have each student draw a name and bring a card or a small wrapped gift for that person.

10. Organize a caroling party. Look for collections of Christmas carols in your library, and practice singing as many of them as you can. Then sing them for other people to enjoy. For example, you might visit other classrooms, a pre-school or day-care center, a hospital, senior center, offices on campus, etc.

11. Interview someone at the police department about the many problems caused by drunk driving during the holidays.

12. Lead the class in singing *Oh Christmas Tree, Oh Come All Ye*

Faithful, Rock of Ages or *Auld Lang Syne.* The words and music are provided in the Appendix.

VIII. Debate It

Form debate teams that argue *pro* or *con* on the following topics. After listening to the teams' arguments, students in the rest of the class may ask questions of the teams, and then vote *pro* or *con* in secret ballot.

1. An adult should have the choice to drink alcohol.

2. It is good for children to believe in "magical" characters such as Santa Claus.

3. Public schools should allow prayer, Christmas celebrations or any other religious activities students and their families request.

4. Debate a topic you choose that relates to this unit. State the idea in one sentence so that people can argue pro or con.

IX. Consider the Proverbs

Guess what each of these sayings means. Then, give an example that illustrates each one. Be prepared to share it with the class. Does your native language have any of the same proverbs? If so, compare them.

1. Don't look a gift horse in the mouth.
2. It is better to give than to receive.
3. Don't judge a book by its cover.
4. Today is the first day of the rest of your life.
5. Don't put off until tomorrow what you can do today.

APPENDIX

The Songs

Transcriptions by Joe Weed

Make New Friends

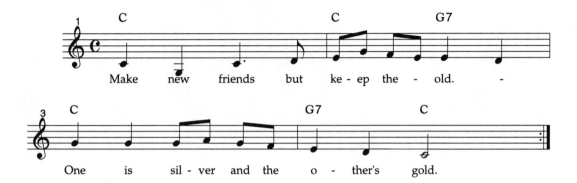

Make New Friends
Sing as a round:

• In two parts, second group begins when first group sings measure 3.

• In three parts, the second group begins when the first group sings measure 2, and the third group begins when the second group sings measure 2.

Sing the song several times.

Happy Birthday

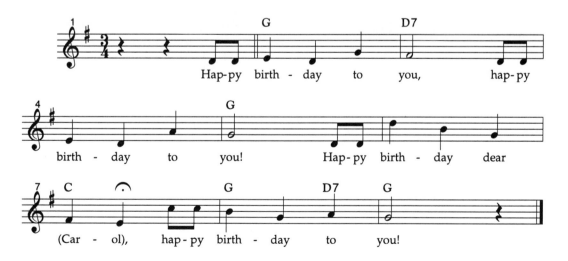

ABC's

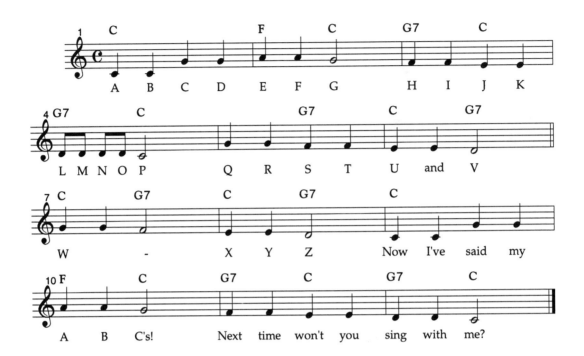

Let My People Go

The Star-Spangled Banner

Francis Scott Key

Over the River

Oh, Christmas Tree

Oh, Christ - mas tree, oh, Christ - mas tree, thy

leaves are so un - chang - ing. Oh, Christ - mas tree, oh,

Christ - mas tree, thy leaves are so un - chang - ing. Not

on - ly green when sum - mer's here, but al - so when it's

cold and drear. Oh, Christ - mas tree, oh, Christ - mas tree, thy

leaves are so un - chang - ing.

Oh, Come All Ye Faithful

Rock of Ages

Auld Lang Syne